VIRGINITY

VIRGINITY

A positive approach to Celibacy for
the sake of the Kingdom of Heaven

Raniero Cantalamessa, OFM Cap

Translated by Charles Serignat

ST PAULS

Library of Congress Cataloging-in-Publication Data

Cantalamessa, Raniero.
    [Verginità. English]
    Virginity : a positive approach to celibacy for the sake
    of the Kingdom of Heaven / Raniero Cantalamessa;
translated by Charles Serignat.
        p.   cm.
    ISBN 0-8189-0745-2
    1. Virginity — Religious aspects — Christianity.
    2. Celibacy —
Religious aspects — Christianity.   I. Title.
BV4647.C.5C3213   1995
248.4'7 — dc20   95-32603
                                          CIP

Produced and designed in the United States of America
by the Fathers and Brothers of the Society of St. Paul,
2187 Victory Boulevard, Staten Island, New York 10314
as part of their communications apostolate.

ISBN: 978-0-8189-0745-6

Printing Information:

Current Printing - first digit   7 8 9 10 11 12

Year of Current Printing - first year shown

            2017 2018 2019 2020 2021 2021 2022 2023

*"There are some who choose not to marry
for the sake of the Kingdom of Heaven.
Let anyone accept this who can."*

(Mt 19:12)

*"God wants celibacy because He wants to be loved…
I need something majestic to love…
There was, and still is, in my soul a need for majesty,
which I shall never grow tired of adoring."*

(S. Kierkegaard, The Journals XI A 154)

Biblical Abbreviations

OLD TESTAMENT

Genesis	Gn	Nehemiah	Ne	Baruch	Ba
Exodus	Ex	Tobit	Tb	Ezekiel	Ezk
Leviticus	Lv	Judith	Jdt	Daniel	Dn
Numbers	Nb	Esther	Est	Hosea	Ho
Deuteronomy	Dt	1 Maccabees	1 M	Joel	Jl
Joshua	Jos	2 Maccabees	2 M	Amos	Am
Judges	Jg	Job	Jb	Obadiah	Ob
Ruth	Rt	Psalms	Ps	Jonah	Jon
1 Samuel	1 S	Proverbs	Pr	Micah	Mi
2 Samuel	2 S	Ecclesiastes	Ec	Nahum	Na
1 Kings	1 K	Song of Songs	Sg	Habakkuk	Hab
2 Kings	2 K	Wisdom	Ws	Zephaniah	Zp
1 Chronicles	1 Ch	Sirach	Si	Haggai	Hg
2 Chronicles	2 Ch	Isaiah	Is	Malachi	Ml
Ezra	Ezr	Jeremiah	Jr	Zechariah	Zc
		Lamentations	Lm		

NEW TESTAMENT

Matthew	Mt	Ephesians	Eph	Hebrews	Heb
Mark	Mk	Philippians	Ph	James	Jm
Luke	Lk	Colossians	Col	1 Peter	1 P
John	Jn	1 Thessalonians	1 Th	2 Peter	2 P
Acts	Ac	2 Thessalonians	2 Th	1 John	1 Jn
Romans	Rm	1 Timothy	1 Tm	2 John	2 Jn
1 Corinthians	1 Cor	2 Timothy	2 Tm	3 John	3 Jn
2 Corinthians	2 Cor	Titus	Tt	Jude	Jude
Galatians	Gal	Philemon	Phm	Revelation	Rv

Table of Contents

Introduction

This book is about virginity and celibacy for the sake of the Kingdom of Heaven. But virginity or celibacy, as well as being a counsel addressed to some, is also, though differently, a precept for everyone. In fact, besides being a freely-chosen, lifelong state, it is also a duty — or rather, an ideal and an evangelical proposal — for everyone during at least one particular phase of life, namely the one preceding the definitive choice of one's vocation.

In this sense these words are not addressed exclusively to religious or to those preparing to become priests, but to all the baptized. We shall find that the same reasons which justify virginity for the sake of the Kingdom can also sustain and motivate the efforts of young Christian men or women to preserve their physical and spiritual chastity and integrity until their wedding day. If virginity is that which enables the consecrated person to say to Christ: "My most exquisite fruits I have reserved for You, my Love" (cf. Sg 7:14), it is also true that to keep oneself chaste with a view to marriage makes it possible, on the wedding day, to give the beloved a priceless gift (secretly desired by everyone) — the gift of hearing those same words addressed to oneself in their most literal sense: "I have reserved my most exquisite fruits for you, my love."

In any case, one cannot speak about virginity and celibacy without continually comparing it with marriage. Therefore to speak about them is also to speak about marriage; in fact in some aspects, comparing the two is the best way to discover the nature and goodness of the charism proper to each.

Today we are witnessing a real attack by the dominant culture against this value of virginity. According to the well-known tendency to despise what one has lost or is unable to attain (as the fox in the fable said of the grapes: "They are not yet ripe"), secular culture casts suspicion and even ridicule on this traditional value which nature itself defends by surrounding it with the delicate yet sturdy safeguard of modesty. Young men and women are pressured by their surroundings —often even by the school environment which ought to help them mature — to be ashamed of their chastity, to do everything to hide it, even to boast about experiences they have not had, simply so as not to appear different from other people. Someone has said that hypocrisy used to be the tribute paid by vice to virtue. Today it is the tribute paid by virtue to vice.

The effect of this mindless assault has been indirectly felt within the Church as well. Nor could it be otherwise, since we live in the world and breathe its air. Whether we go out or stay at home, we are besieged and "de-evangelized" on every side and by every means. Celibacy and virginity, it is sometimes said, prevent healthy, complete personal development. They keep a man from being fully a man, and a woman from being fully a woman. One consequence of this is apparent in the way we present our vocational material. Sometimes at vocation meetings I have had the impression that the invitation to follow a call to special consecration is made with this tacit but clear implication: "Embrace our way of life *despite* the fact that it involves celibacy or virginity; actually, you will be able to contribute to the coming of the Kingdom, help the poor, raise people's awareness, live without being enslaved to things, and promote social justice." I believe that we must acknowledge our lack of faith and have the courage to invite young people to embrace our consecrated life not *despite* the virginity and celibacy it entails, but *because* of them, or at least *also* because of them. This ideal may very well be the one that will cause young people to fall in love with the religious and priestly life and draw them to it, rather than distance them from it. It has happened before; it happened in the first ages of the Church.

The fact is that virginity for the Kingdom is a splendid value which changing times and fashions cannot alter. All the forces and wisdom of this world, all the so-called human sciences may join together in protest against this form of life, calling it "an outdated abomination" and raising all kinds of suspicion against it; all the sins and infidelities of the very people who have chosen to embrace it may be added to this, and still it would remain, because it was instituted by Jesus. No one will ever be able to uproot that which the Son of God planted with His own hand when He came into the world.

The world itself, without realizing it, pays its own tribute to this value when it uses the words "virgin" and "pure" in a very positive way. An unspoiled landscape is often described as "virgin," the best wool is labelled "pure," and so on. We need to reclaim these words and symbols which our secularized culture has borrowed from the Bible and Christian tradition and emptied completely of their religious meaning.

In an age like our own, when sexual excesses threaten the very sources of life and the basis of society itself, when nature protests with dire warning signals, it is a duty and a joy for believers to rediscover the radical alternative of the Gospel. This alternative does not rule out sex, but brings out its human, free, rational character, preventing it from degenerating into sheer instinct and banality. The poet Tagore, expressing an evangelical insight, writes: "Chastity is a wealth that comes from *abundance of love*" (not from the lack of it).

VIRGINITY

PART ONE

The Biblical Motivations for
Virginity and Celibacy for the Sake
of the Kingdom of Heaven

1. "THERE ARE SOME WHO CHOOSE
   NOT TO MARRY FOR THE SAKE
   OF THE KINGDOM OF HEAVEN."

I will speak interchangeably of celibacy, virginity and voluntary continence, because they are all terms designating the same actual reality, or at least the same state of life. Personally I prefer to use the word "virginity" and "virgins" as the most comprehensive term. In fact the New Testament does not reserve this title only for unmarried women, but also uses it for unmarried men. The Book of Revelation gives the name "virgins" to those who have not been with women and who therefore follow the Lamb wherever He goes (cf. Rv 14:4).

The institution of this state is described in chapter 19 of Matthew's Gospel: "His disciples said to Him: 'If that's how things are between husband and wife, it's better not to marry.' But He replied: 'Not everyone can accept what I have said, but only those to whom it is granted. For there are some who are eunuchs from their mother's womb, and some who were made so by other men, and there are eunuchs who have made themselves so for the sake of the Kingdom of Heaven. Let anyone accept this who can'" (Mt 19:10-12).

The word "eunuch" sounds rather harsh to our modern ears and it was harsh also for people in Jesus'

5

day. According to some, the choice of this unusual term was due to the fact that the adversaries of Jesus had accused Him of being a eunuch, since He was unmarried, just as they accused Him on other occasions of being a glutton and a drunkard (cf. Mt 11:19). It was a highly offensive word, because for the Jewish mentality of the time it was a moral duty to get married. The opinion of a certain Rabbi Eleazar, according to which "a man with no wife is not even a man,"[1] is well known. So here, Jesus was taking up His adversaries' accusation and making it in some way His own, but explaining it by this revelation of an unmarried state that was new and absolutely special.

There are some — says Jesus — "who do not marry" (this is the non-polemical equivalent of the term "eunuch") because they are prevented from birth on account of some natural defect. Others do not marry because they are prevented by the wickedness of people or the circumstances of life. Finally, there are others again who do not marry for the sake of the Kingdom of Heaven. In the last case the word "eunuch" takes on a different significance, not physical but moral. Christian tradition has always interpreted it in this way except for the well-known case of Origen who, contrary to his custom of explaining everything spiritually, took this word of the Gospel literally. He castrated himself and subsequently paid a high price for his mistake.

The mention of the Kingdom of Heaven abruptly introduces an element of mystery into Jesus' words, which is heightened by the final laconic phrase: "Let anyone accept this who can." In other words, those who have received the gift of understanding will understand.

In this way a second state of life is born into the world, and this is its "Magna Charta." In fact, before Jesus, no state of life existed comparable to this one instituted by Him, at least in its motivation if not in fact. The Essenes of Qumran also knew and practiced a form of celibacy, but for them it had undertones of asceticism and ritual purity rather than eschatological connotations. If anything, it was motivated by an expectation of the Kingdom, not by its coming. In any case it could not have been otherwise. Only the presence of the Kingdom on earth could institute this second possibility: a life of celibacy "for the sake of the Kingdom." This possibility does not cancel out the other one, namely marriage, but makes it relative. The same sort of thing happens with the idea of the state in the political sphere: the revelation of the simultaneous presence in history of the Kingdom of God does not abolish the state, but radically relativizes it. Perfect continence stands in the face of marriage rather as the Kingdom of God stands in the face of the kingdom of Caesar: it does not eliminate it, but highlights the different position it now has from the one it had before. It is no longer the only instance in its field. Since God's

Kingdom is in a different order of greatness from that of Caesar, the one does not need to deny the other in order to exist. In the same way, voluntary continence does not need the denial of marriage for its own validity to be recognized. In fact, it is only by simultaneously affirming marriage — especially since Jesus raised it to the dignity of a sacrament — that chastity acquires meaning.

The prophetic dimension of Virginity and Celibacy

In order to understand this new form of life and its deepest justification, we need to start from the motivation adopted by Jesus Himself: "for the sake of the Kingdom of Heaven." The nature of virginity and celibacy and their justification depend on the nature of the Kingdom of Heaven itself. ("Kingdom of Heaven" is the expression Matthew uses for "Kingdom of God." Being a good Jew, he wanted to avoid mentioning God directly, but it means the same thing.) Now the Kingdom of God has the characteristic of being, as we say today in a very appropriate formula, "already" and "not yet." It is "already" here, it has come, it is present. The Kingdom of Heaven — says Jesus — is close at hand, it is among you. But in another sense the Kingdom of Heaven has not yet arrived, it is still to come, and this is why we pray "Thy kingdom come."

Since the Kingdom of Heaven has already come, because with Christ final salvation is operative in the world, therefore — and here is the conclusion that concerns us — it is possible for some people, called by God, to choose even now to live as people do in the final condition of the Kingdom. And how does one live in the final condition of the Kingdom? Jesus Himself tells us in Luke's Gospel: "The children of this world marry and are given in marriage, but those who are counted worthy of *that* age and resurrection from the dead neither marry nor are given in marriage, because they are no longer able to die — they're angel-like and are children of God, since they've attained the resurrection" (Lk 20:34-36; cf. also Mt 22:30).

It is precisely in this that the prophetic dimension of virginity and celibacy for the sake of the Kingdom resides. By the simple fact that it exists, without the need for words, this form of life shows what the final condition of men and women will be: one that is destined to last for ever. It is a prophetic existence. There has been much discussion in the past about whether virginity is a more perfect state than marriage, and if so in what sense. I believe that it is not *ontologically* (that is, in itself) *a more perfect state*, but it is an *eschatologically more advanced* state, in the sense that it is more like the definitive state towards which we are all journeying. "You have begun to be what we shall be," wrote St. Cyprian to the first Christian virgins.[2]

Such a prophecy, far from being against married people, is actually first of all for them, for their benefit. It reminds them that marriage is holy, beautiful, and redeemed by Christ. It is the image of the betrothal of Christ to the Church, but… it is not everything. It is a reality that is linked to this world and therefore transitory. It no longer exists where death no longer exists. When, as Jesus said, it will no longer be possible to die, there will be no more need to marry (cf. Lk 20:36).

For married people, virginity is a reminder of the primacy of the spirit and of God. It reminds them that God has made us for Himself and that therefore our hearts will always be "unsatisfied," until they rest in Him. It is a reminder, too, that marriage and the family cannot be turned into an idol to which everything and everyone is sacrificed, a kind of absolute in life. Everyone knows how easy it is to hide behind one's family duties ("I have a wife and children") in order to avoid the radical demands of the Gospel, and how easy it is to make a good marriage the supreme ideal and purpose in life, even using its success to measure the success of one's own life. And since the first casualty of such undue absolutization is marriage itself, which is crushed by these disproportionate expectations which it will never be able to satisfy, this is why I say that virginity comes to the aid of married people themselves. It liberates marriage and each of the partners from the unbearable weight of having to be "everything" for the other, of taking the place of God. The eschatological reservations that virginity places upon marriage do not lessen its joy; rather, they save it from despair, because they open up for marriage a horizon stretching even beyond death. Precisely because eternity and a heavenly Jerusalem exist, a married couple who love each other know that their communion is not destined to end with this passing world and dissolve into nothing, but that, transfigured and spiritualized, it will last for eternity.

Starting from this prophetic character of virginity and celibacy we can understand how ambiguous and wrong is the claim that this state is against nature and prevents men and women from being fully themselves, i.e. fully men and women. We have let ourselves be influenced by all the talk raised against it in the name of psychology and psychoanalysis. Doubt weighs heavily on the soul of young people and it can be one of the main reasons why they are reluctant to respond to a vocation. We have not always remembered that this modern science has often been built upon a materialistic and atheistic view of the human person. Therefore, what it says in this field can have a certain weight for someone who does not believe in the existence of God and of a life after death, but for someone who does believe in these things it has no weight at all. The difference between the two positions has been thought to be negligible, whereas it is decisive. In reality, virginity makes sense precisely because eternal life and the risen state exist. It is a reality of the Spirit, and what Paul says about the things of the Spirit apply to it, namely, that "the unspiritual person is unable to accept what comes from the Spirit of God, since for him it's foolishness. He's unable to understand such matters because they can only be evaluated spiritually" (cf. 1 Cor 2:14). For a person of faith to expect the opposite from an unbeliever would be almost as great a folly as the first.

Writing to a friend who was also convinced that to choose chastity would be to cut himself off from the mainstream of life, Paul Claudel replied in these enlightening words: "We are still living with the old romantic illusion that the highest happiness, the great significance, the only romance in life, consist in our relationships with women and in the sensual satisfactions we derive from them. We forget only one thing: that the soul and the spirit are just as real and strong and demanding as the flesh — they are much more so! — and that if we allow the flesh everything it asks for, this is to the detriment of other joys, other marvellous realms, which will remain closed to us for ever. We empty a glass of poor wine in a sleazy pub or saloon, and forget this virginal sea which others are contemplating under the rising sun."[3]

Psychoanalysis itself, once it has overcome the basic prejudice inherited from its founder and opens up to the spiritual and eternal dimension of the person, rediscovers the extraordinary value of virginity as a sign. "The only way out of human conflict" — these are the words of one of the first and most famous disciples of Freud — "is full renunciation, to give one's life as a gift to the highest powers ... The true heroic validation of one's life lies beyond sex, beyond the private religion — all these are makeshifts that pull him down or that hem him in, leaving him torn with ambiguity... And in order to get such centering, man has to look beyond the 'thou,' beyond the consolations of others and of the things of this world."[4]

But we can reach the same conclusion by an even more certain route, that of revelation, and we can see how virginity and celibacy do not deny nature, but only fulfill it at a deeper level. Human thought, in order to find out what human beings are and what is "natural" to them, has always based itself on an analysis of human nature, understanding by nature — according to the etymological meaning of the word — what human beings are and have from birth. The Bible on the other hand (which knows nothing of any concept of nature as applied to humanity) bases itself on the concept of *vocation*: men and women are not only what they are by nature, but also what they are called to become by using their freedom and in obedience to God's word. The perfect human being is the risen Jesus, the "second man," the "last Adam" (cf. 1 Cor 15:45-47), as the Church Fathers said. The more a person approaches this model of humanity, the more truly and fully human he or she is. If nature were all there was, there would be no valid motive to oppose natural tendencies and impulses. But there is also vocation. In a certain sense we could say that the most "natural" state for a person is precisely virginity, because we are not called to live in an eternal relationship as a couple, but to live in an eternal relationship with God. God, and not a human partner, is destined to be our "all" forever (cf. 1 Cor 15:28).

The missionary dimension of Celibacy and Virginity

This is the first motive for virginity and celibacy, deriving from the fact that the Kingdom has already come. Let us now go back to the foundational words of Jesus to discover the second motive: it, too, is inherent in the nature of the Kingdom. We were saying that, in another sense, the Kingdom of God has "not yet" come, it is on the way. It has to come in *intensity* within the Church (how many areas inside ourselves are still pagan and need to be evangelized!). It must come *in extension*, until it reaches the ends of the earth. How many nations and entire continents are still waiting for the light of the Gospel!

Now here is the motive that flows from this: since God's Kingdom has not yet come but is on the way, we need men and women who will devote themselves full-time and wholeheartedly to the coming of that Kingdom. And this brings us to the missionary or apostolic dimension of virginity and celibacy, which flows quite obviously and without any forcing from Jesus' words "for the sake of the Kingdom of Heaven." It concerns not only those consecrated people who actually go to far away countries to proclaim the Gospel, but all virgins, all unmarried men and women. The Church has recognized this fact by proclaiming a cloistered nun, Saint Thérèse of the Child Jesus, Co-Patron of the Missions.

It is difficult to imagine what the Church would be like today had there not been, through the centuries, this host of men and women who have left "house, wife or children" for the sake of the Kingdom of Heaven (cf. Lk 18:29). The proclamation of the Gospel and mission work have rested to a large extent on their shoulders. Within Christianity, they have promoted knowledge of the Word of God through study; they have opened up new ways of Christian thought and spirituality; abroad, they have carried the message of the Kingdom to the most remote peoples. They are the ones who brought into being nearly all the charitable institutions that have so enriched the Church and the world.

Sometimes the Catholic Church is accused of having put too wide an interpretation on the words of Jesus about voluntary celibacy for the sake of the Kingdom, by imposing it on all its priests. It is true that Jesus did not impose the choice of celibacy, but neither does the Church impose it, much less does it forbid anyone to marry. To view the celibacy of Catholic priests in this light is a grave distortion. The Church has only laid this down as one of the requirements for those who wish to exercise the priestly ministry, which remains a free choice. The Church copies Jesus' approach to the rich young man and says: If you want to work with me, accept a life of chastity and then come and serve me. "If you want!" Since the priesthood is a call to serve the Church as fellow-workers of the Bishop, it surely has the right to determine the requirements for such service. It is the identical principle followed by the Orthodox Church in reserving the episcopate to unmarried men. The difference between the Catholic and Orthodox Churches lies not in the principle itself, but only in the extent of its application. It seems to me, therefore, that there is a much more serious failure by default, in the case of those Christian churches which lack any form of this evangelical proposal in practice, namely, of celibacy for the Kingdom, as if Jesus had never mentioned the subject and it was simply a later invention by the Church. In the same way also they often lack any practical form of the other equally clear and explicit proposal to sell everything in order to follow Christ in voluntary poverty. In these circumstances, I wonder how it is still possible to speak of the "full Gospel." It may indeed be a full Gospel, but it is full of... holes. Since it is not of divine origin, the compulsory celibacy of priests is open to discussion, but no one can honestly deny that despite all the difficulties and defections that are inevitable in a matter of this kind, the choice made by the Church has, overall, enormously benefitted the cause of the Kingdom and of holiness and is a most effective sign among the Christian people today.

It is apparent from everything we have said that virginity does not mean sterility. On the contrary, it signifies the utmost *fruitfulness*, obviously on a different, higher level than the physical. The first time virginity appears in salvation history, it is associated with the birth of a child: "A virgin shall conceive and bear a son" (Is 7:14). Tradition has noted this link and constantly associates the title of virgin with that of mother. Mary is the virgin mother; the Church is both virgin and mother. "The Father of all is one" — writes Clement of Alexandria — "and the Word of all is one, and one and the same is the Holy Spirit, and one alone is the virgin mother: this is how I like to address the Church."[5] Finally, each soul, particularly each consecrated soul, is a virgin and mother: "Every faithful soul, spouse of the Word of God, mother, daughter and sister of Christ, is understood to be a virgin with her own form of fertility."[6]

It is a matter, as I said, of a different kind of fruitfulness — a fruitfulness of the spirit, not of the body. And since human beings are spirit as well as flesh, it is also a supremely human fruitfulness, a case of truly becoming a father or mother. It is the same kind of fruitfulness that enabled St. Paul to say to the Christians he himself had instructed in the faith: "It was I who fathered you in Christ Jesus" (1 Cor 4:15), and again: "My children, I am going through the pain of giving birth to you all over again" (Gal 4:19). The Christian people know this very well: in every culture they have spontaneously given to virgin men — priests, religious, monks — the title of father, and to virgin women the title of mother. How many missionaries and founders of charities are remembered simply as "the Father," and how many women known simply as "the Mother."

Today there is a great deal of talk about the "quality of life." It is said that the most important thing is not to increase the quantity of life on our planet, but to raise its quality. By "quality" people generally mean the quality of hygiene, health care or culture. But there is also a spiritual quality of life, which is the most important, because it concerns the human soul — what remains of a person in eternity. Those who are virgins for the sake of the Kingdom are called to spend all their energies in raising this spiritual quality of life — quite apart from the fact that they are often the ones who do most, in the best and most disinterested way, to raise the other quality of life, in hygiene, health care and culture.

St. Gregory Nazianzen wrote a splendid verse in praise of virginity. At first when I read it I thought the language was rather overdone, aimed at extolling the value of virginity. What it actually says is that there is a model for virginity that is higher than the Church, higher even than Mary: the Trinity! "The first Virgin," he says, "is the holy Trinity."[7] On further reflection I found, once again, that the Fathers never say anything just for the sake of it, without an objective and profound reason. Yes, the first virgin really is the holy Trinity, not just because the first generation of the Word by the Father is virginal, but also because the Trinity created the universe alone, without the aid of any other principle, not even some kind of "pre-existing matter." It created out of nothing, virginally. In every act of sexual procreation there is an element of selfishness and desire. When a man and woman produce a child, they give a gift, certainly, but they also "gift each other." They fulfill themselves, but they also "fulfill each other." They need the encounter with the other for their own fulfillment and enrichment. On the other hand, when the Trinity creates, it confers fulfillment. Since it is already perfectly happy and complete in itself, it has no need of further fulfillment. "You have created all things" says Eucharistic Prayer IV, "to fill your creatures with every blessing and lead all men to the joyful vision of your light."

Here, virginity shows its most beautiful characteristic, which is gratuity. Christian virgin men and women imitate this gratuity to some degree when they love and care for children who are not their own according to the flesh, nurse the sick people of others, care for other people's old folk, and when — especially in the case of the Church's cloistered monks and nuns — they carry the weight of other people's sins, bringing them before God in intercession for the world. "At certain hours of the day and night" — we read in a medieval Rule for cloistered women — "hold in your hearts all the sick and afflicted who suffer pain or poverty, and think of the torments endured by those lying in prison in heavy iron fetters... With hearts full of compassion, think of those undergoing grave trials. Keep in your hearts the pains of all these people, and ask Our Lord with sighs to have mercy on them and to turn His merciful countenance towards them."[8] Certainly such a life cannot be called sterile when it is lived with a vision as broad as the world itself.

The virgin's fruitfulness is spousal in nature. Children are begotten through union with a spouse, and in fact the virgin, "living for the Lord without distractions," as St. Paul would say, brings forth children for Christ. When we priests come across souls so sunk in evil that we are unable to bring them back to the light alone, to whom do we turn? We knock at the door of some convent of nuns and entrust the person to a bride of Christ. Time and again in such cases we witness the miracle of a resurrection, even though we will never know (God alone knows) what that miracle has cost. One day, when these virgins set foot in the heavenly Jerusalem and meet those sons and daughters they never knew they had, they too will exclaim in amazement, like the virgin Sion: "Who has borne me these? I was bereft and barren; who has reared these?" (Is 49:21).

The fruitfulness of the cloistered virgin depends on the fact that, by prayer, silent faith, hope and love, she acts directly on the primary cause, which is God, not on the secondary causes. And it is the Bridegroom Who distributes her fruits to His friends. With the bride in the Song of Songs, she says to Christ: "My most exquisite fruits I have reserved for you, my Love" (cf. Sg 7:14). And the Bridegroom answers: "I come into my garden, my sister, my promised bride, I pick my myrrh and balsam." Then, turning to sinners, He says: "Eat, friends, and drink, drink deep, my dearest friends" (Sg 5:1). The bride does not wish to know who is to benefit from the fruits of her prayers and sufferings. They belong to the Bridegroom, Who gives them to whom He will. Others will have to worry about how to distribute and administer them. It is not her concern. Truly, the Lord "lets the barren woman be seated at home, the happy mother of children" (Ps 113:9).

2. "The unmarried give their minds to the Lord's affairs."

The second great New Testament text on virginity, alongside Matthew 19, is to be found in St. Paul's First Letter to the Corinthians. He says: "This world as we know it is passing away! I want you to be free from anxiety. The unmarried man concerns himself with the Lord's affairs, with how to please the Lord, while the married man concerns himself with worldly affairs — how to please his wife — and he is divided. Likewise, girls who are betrothed and unmarried women are concerned with the Lord's affairs — how to be holy in body and spirit — while a married woman is concerned with affairs of the world, such as how to please her husband. I am saying this for your own good, not simply to rein you in — I want you to preserve good order so you'll be able to devote yourselves to the Lord without distractions" (1 Cor 7:31-35).

At first sight, the motivation St. Paul gives for virginity seems different from that given by Jesus. It appears subjective, almost psychological, centered more on the good of individuals and their peace of mind than on the Kingdom of God. But this is not the case. It is the same exquisitely objective and theological motive which has God as its aim, not oneself. All the motives adopted by the Apostle for virginity are summed up in the expression "for the Lord," and ever since Easter this is the exact equivalent of the expression: "for the Kingdom of Heaven." We know that, after Easter, the expression "Kingdom of Heaven" or "Kingdom of God," so central in the preaching of Jesus, disappears almost completely from Christian preaching. In its place we find the apostolic proclamation: "Christ has died; He is risen; He is Lord!" Indeed, now the Kingdom, or salvation, consists precisely in that fact. Before Easter Jesus said: "The appointed time has come and the Kingdom of God is close at hand. Repent, and believe in the good news!" (Mk 1:15). After Easter, this fundamental proclamation, made up of a piece of news ("The Kingdom is at hand!") and a command ("Repent"), now sounds like this: "This Jesus whom you crucified God made both Lord and Messiah... repent and be baptized in the name of Jesus Christ for the forgiveness of your sins" (Ac 2:36, 38).

The motive Paul uses to justify his exhortation to virginity — "This world as we know it is passing away!" — sounds very much like the one we looked at above, namely that "the appointed time has come" — these are now the end times in which it is possible to live already as "children of the resurrection" in the manner of the world to come.

However, there is one difference between the two texts (Jesus' and Paul's) and it is important to note it. According to Jesus, a person may remain unmarried "for the sake of the Kingdom of Heaven," i.e. for *a cause*; according to Paul, marriage is renounced "for the sake of the Lord," i.e., for a *person*. This represents a progression in the idea of virginity — not one due to St. Paul, but to Jesus Himself Who, by dying and rising for us, has become "the Lord," the Bridegroom and Head of the Church, the One Who "loved the Church and gave Himself up for her to sanctify her by cleansing her with water and the word. In this way He'll be able to present the Church to Himself in all its glory, having neither stain nor wrinkle nor anything of that sort, but instead holy and unblemished" (Eph 5:25-27).

Now let us examine a little more closely what the Apostle says about virginity. He starts by saying that he would like to see his faithful people "free from anxiety" (*amerimnous*). If you stop there, there is a danger of seeing virginity and celibacy as a wonderful opportunity for a tranquil life, with no problems or worries. Like St. Peter who, hearing Jesus that day proclaiming the austere demands of marriage, said: "If *that's* the way things are between husband and wife, it's better not to marry!" (cf. Mt 19:10). Jesus too thought it better not to marry, but for a very different reason from the self-regarding one understood by Peter, as He immediately explains by talking about those who do not marry for the sake of the Kingdom of Heaven.

Who, after all, would not sign up for a care-free life? In St. Paul's day the Stoics and Epicureans also followed a similar ideal which they called apatheia, or *atarassìa*, meaning to live a life without emotional or affective upheavals, being ready to sacrifice everything to this ideal, even joys and pleasures that were too intense.

But we must pay close attention to what the Apostle immediately adds: "The unmarried [person] concerns himself with [literally, "gives his mind to" (*merimnà*)] the Lord's affairs." Here is a remarkable contrast and a paradox. Paul has just said that he wants his children to be "free from all anxiety," and now he says that he wants them to be full of concern, and he says so twice, once to unmarried men and once to unmarried women. So, they, too, are to be preoccupied, but "with the Lord's affairs." This is not the ideal of a tranquil, impassive, untroubled life. It does mean living without worldly concerns, so as to have all the time and leisure available to devote to the Lord's affairs.

What, then, are the "Lord's affairs" which must concerned them? Parish matters or property concerns? The so-called "goods of the Church"? The goods, or affairs, of the Lord are the souls He died for: the Kingdom. This is why celibates and virgins exist: so that there will be someone, in the Church and in the world, who is concerned solely for God's interests.

Nor is it true that such people do not marry. Virgins are not people who renounce marriage. They are people who renounce life-long commitment to a *creature*. This becomes true and obvious for virgins from the moment when they make the personal discovery of Jesus as "Lord" of their life, and realize that this Lord is not Someone Who belongs only to the past (when He was on earth), or only to the future (when we too will be with Him in Heaven), but that, in virtue of His resurrection He is alive "in the Spirit" and is present at every moment in His Church. So it is not a question of a virgin man or woman renouncing a "concrete" love for the sake of an "abstract" one, a real person for an imaginary one. It is a matter of renouncing one concrete love for another concrete love, one real person for Another Who is infinitely more real. The difference is that in one case the union is "according to the flesh," in the other "according to the Spirit"; in one case the couple form "one flesh," in the other, they form "one spirit." Indeed it is written that "anyone who attaches himself to the Lord is one spirit with Him" (1 Cor 6:17). According to an ancient antiphon in the liturgy of her feast, it was this realism in faith that made Saint Agnes say, when she was faced with a proposal of human marriage: "I am already married ... My Lord Jesus Christ has bound me to Himself with a ring."

Therefore, celibates and virgins for the sake of the Kingdom are not simply people who have "renounced marriage." Rather, they are people who mysteriously (we are talking about a gift!) and at times even painfully have realized — perhaps after having made the attempt — that another person, a family, children, all of these were not enough for them. They felt "too confined" by them, they needed something divine to love. There was once a great man who found that he had to accept such an invitation from God on his own, outside of any structure or institution, in a Protestant, Lutheran environment which he found hostile and suspicious of such a choice. (Luther, remember, had rejected celibacy and virginity and chosen marriage.) He was engaged to a girl called Regina, whom he loved as only a young man gifted with his idealism could love — we are talking about Sören Kierkegaard. Once he understood what his true mission was, and what his life in the world would be like, he faced the martyrdom of breaking up with her. In fact, he did all he could to ensure that she would be the one to leave him, acting in such a way that people thought him disloyal and contemptible. Toward the end of his life, writing in his *Diary*, he justified his choice in words which add something new to all the tributes, ancient or modern, that I know of in praise of celibacy and virginity. I hope there will be someone to whom these words will come as a sudden revelation of their vocation: "God," he writes, "wants celibacy, because He wants to be loved... O infinite Majesty, even if You were not love, even if You were aloof in Your infinite majesty, I still could not help loving You, for I need something majestic to love. What others have complained of — namely that they did not find love in this world, and therefore felt the need to love You, since You are love (which I agree with

27

totally) — I would like to proclaim too, and apply it to the majestic. There was, and still is, in my soul a need for majesty, which I shall never grow tired or weary of adoring. In the world I found nothing of this majesty for which I yearned."[9] Spouses of God's majesty! Spouses of the Absolute!

In truth I believe that there is no better word than the verb "to espouse," to express this new and special relationship which virginity establishes with Christ and with God, even leaving aside all the mystical significance usually associated with this term in religious language. We say of someone metaphorically that they have "espoused" a cause when they have given themselves wholly to it, body and soul, making the interests, risks and success of that cause their own. In this sense we are entitled to say that the virgin has espoused the Kingdom or the Lord, but to a much greater degree, because virginity is not just espousing a "cause," but also a person; not just for a time, but for eternity. The bond that binds the celibate and the virgin to the Lord is so total, so exclusive, that its only equivalent on the human level is when a man marries a woman.

Rabbi Simeon ben Azzai, a Jewish rabbi who lived at the time of St. Paul and was a keen student of the Mosaic Law, challenged the commonly accepted notions of his fellow countrymen by refusing to marry. He gave this justification: "My soul is in love with the Torah. Others will make sure that the world survives!"[10] With all the more reason, the Christian celibate or virgin can make these words their own and say: "My soul is in love with Jesus Christ. Others will make sure that the world survives!"

Having espoused the *cause* of the Kingdom of Heaven, we are called to *serve* that cause; having married a *person*, the Lord, we are called to *please* that person. "The unmarried person," St. Paul says, "is concerned with the Lord's affairs, with *how to please the Lord*." This is more than just simple service! Is a wife supposed to please her husband? Is that her dearest wish? Well, so is the virgin meant to please Someone! The Apostle, by talking in this way about the married and the unmarried, is tacitly inviting the Christian virgin to follow the example of the married person. Is there anything a fiance would not do to please his fiancee, and vice versa? Or a faithful wife, to please her husband, and vice versa? The Christian virgin is to have that same instinctive need, that constant disposition, to please the Lord. Only the means of "pleasing" are different. St. Peter recalls some that apply to all women of faith, but even more to Christian virgins: "Don't try to be beautiful by braiding your hair, wearing gold jewelry, and putting on fine clothing. Instead, let your beauty be that of the person hidden in your heart, the imperishable beauty of a gentle and quiet spirit, which is precious in the sight of God" (1 P 3:3-4).

The Church Fathers laid much emphasis on this point in their descriptions of what the behavior and adornment of Christian virgins ought to be. St. Cyprian even wrote a treatise on the subject, called *De habitu virginum*. But, in this matter, the virgin has a better Counsellor than the Fathers, One Who helps her discover the tastes and wishes of her Bridegroom: namely, the Holy Spirit! She should entrust herself to Him, then, on this wonderful journey of betrothal.

She needs to know that by doing this, she is fulfilling a task that is not just personal but also ecclesial, not just subjective, but also objective: her job is to be a small *epiphany*, or visible manifestation, of the Church as the Bride of Christ. The Church, in itself and in a general way, has no visible face or a soul endowed with freedom, because it is not a physical but a "mystical person." Who better than the consecrated virgin embodies this quality of being "a pure virgin to be presented to one husband — to Christ" (2 Cor 11:2)? It is true that married people also share in this symbolism, but with a different nuance. Husband and wife are a sign of the "great mystery" of the union between Christ and the Church (cf. Eph 5:32), but separately, in the sense that the husband symbolizes Christ and the wife, the Church, while the virgin, whether man or woman, only represents the Church in her relation to Christ. It is a different kind of symbolism, even though it is highly instructive to see already how both these ways serve as symbols of spiritual realities and are therefore holy.

An undivided heart

There is an idea expressed in our text by St. Paul which we have not yet paid attention to, and that is the idea of an undivided heart. Married people, necessarily concerned with the world's affairs and how to please their spouse, "are divided," whereas virginity enables one to live "devoted to the Lord, without distractions." I said just now that the state of virginity, as St. Paul presents it, is not subjective and psychological in nature, but objective; that it has the Lord as its center and aim, and not personal benefit. Now, we have to say that, in a subordinate way, it also fulfils this second function of personal enhancement and growth. In other words, it does have a strong subjective, existential significance. In fact it helps a person to achieve the finest, most difficult enterprise of all, which is to become inwardly unified.

There is a "diaspora," a dispersion, even within ourselves. If Jesus were to ask me, as He did that poor demoniac in the Gospel: "What is your name?" I too would have to reply: "My name is legion, for there are many of us" (Mk 5:9). There are as many of us as there are desires, plans and regrets which we harbor, each one different from and contrary to others which pull us in opposite directions.

They literally distract us, drag us apart. Virginity is a powerful aid to progress toward interior unity, in virtue of the fact that it enables us to live united to the Lord, and able to devote ourselves to Him "without distractions." United in oneself and united to the Lord — the unity we are talking about consists in precisely these elements. St. Augustine has written: "Through continence, in fact, we are gathered in and returned to the One, from which we have flowed out into the many. For he loves You less who loves something else along with You, which he does not love for Your sake."[11]

This unity is what Jesus calls "purity of heart," and it is realized most of all at the level of the will. It consists in wanting fewer and fewer things, until eventually one wants "one thing only." When a person can truthfully say with the psalmist: "One thing alone have I asked of the Lord, one thing only do I seek" (Ps 27:4), and "Whom else have I in heaven but You? With You, I lack nothing on earth" (Ps 73:25), then such a person is coming close to real virginity of heart, of which physical virginity is the sign and safeguard. This is because virginity of the heart consists in wanting one thing only, that one thing being God.

This illuminating and unifying aspect of virginity was the one that some strongly ascetical and mystical Fathers such as Gregory of Nyssa most liked to emphasize. For him, true virginity is interior, and consists in progressively freeing oneself from passions and desires (*pathe*) in order to unite oneself to God. The other, physical virginity, is strictly related to and in view of the first, a kind of protective wrapping for it. He writes: "In order to contemplate the bliss of the divine pleasure in the best way possible, the liberated soul, once released, must not turn to any earthly thing, or taste any of what are commonly claimed to be pleasures. On the contrary, she transfers the impulse of her love from material things in order to contemplate with her mind what is beautiful in a non-material way. Bodily virginity has been devised precisely so that this disposition of the heart could come about. Its principal function is to make the soul forget the natural movements of the passions, and to prevent the base needs of the flesh from reaching the point where they must be satisfied. The soul, once freed from these, will no longer run the risk of gradually growing used to things apparently permitted by the law of nature, and thus of abandoning or ignoring that divine and genuine pleasure which can only be pursued by the purity of the rational element that guides us."[12]

There is no doubt that there are some married people who are further advanced along this way than many celibates and virgins. Gregory of Nyssa himself, who outlined this marvellous program for interior purity, was married. But this does not take away from the fact that the virgin, as such, is more favored when it comes to this task, and consequently more responsible if he or she is careless about implementing it. Married people must inevitably be concerned with the affairs of the world, of their family. They cannot help being divided. The same Gregory of Nyssa says of the married woman that: "A fragment of her heart goes away with every child she has, and if she has had many children, her soul is divided into as many parts as she has had children, so that she feels in her very depths whatever happens to each of them."[13] Obviously this can become a way for her to grow in holiness ("A woman," says Scripture in 1 Tm 2:15, "will be saved by childbearing"), but this does not take away the fact that she is, in some sense, also divided by childbearing.

Once again, however, on the subject of the undivided heart, we have occasion to reflect and be afraid. The undivided heart is a good thing, as long as you love somebody. In fact, a divided heart that loves someone is better than an undivided heart that loves nobody — the latter would actually be undivided egoism. It would mean having one's heart full, but with the most corrupting thing there is: oneself. Of this type of virgin and celibate, unfortunately none too rare, Charles Péguy has rightly said: "Because they do not belong to someone else, they think they belong to God. Because they love no one else, they think that they love God."

Looked at from any angle, it is clear that the essence of celibacy and virginity for the Kingdom is a spousal love for the Lord. The very "fruitfulness" of this state of life depends on it. Just as a marriage without love would not be a true marriage, even if it was "valid," so would virginity without love hardly be true virginity, only a semblance, a hard and empty shell, without a soul.

The main motive for Christian virginity is therefore positive, not negative. The phenomenology of religion is familiar with many forms of virginity, at least temporary ones, even outside Christianity. But in these cases it either has a negative motive of separation and abstention from the world and material things, as in Gnosticism (whose watchword was "fasting from the world"), or else one of ritual purification—also tending towards the negative — by which children (*pueri innupti*) and vestal virgins, by reason of their uncorrupt state, were considered more worthy to approach God.[14] In this last case we see an example reminiscent of the principle in Jewish Levitical law, of also abstaining from marriage when acts of worship and sacrifices were to be performed.

I have a great love for the Fathers of the Church, but on this point, just for once, I would have a criticism to make. As we have seen, in the New Testament virginity has an essentially positive motivation: the Kingdom, the Lord. In the Fathers, it gradually acquires a predominantly negative and ascetical motivation, namely the renunciation of marriage and liberation from the passions. In the

New Testament, the *motive* ("for the sake of the Kingdom," "for the Lord"), prevails over the *fact* (being unmarried). In the Fathers, the fact of being unmarried tends to prevail over the motive, although this obviously does not disappear. I was speaking earlier about St. Paul's text, of the danger of going no further than the context suggested by the words "free from all anxiety." This did occasionally happen, when the Stoic ideal of *apatheia*, the absence of passion and desire, became the most desirable aspect of the monastic and virginal state.

The treatises of the Fathers on virginity, such as for example St. John Chrysostom's famous one, spend about half the time trying to throw light on the evils in marriage. Chrysostom says: "The slavery of marriage is harsh and inevitable. Even when it is free from all pain, marriage has no greatness in itself: of what advantage could the most perfect of marriages be at the moment of death? None at all!" Even Gregory of Nyssa, although married as I said, feels the need to speak of "the unpleasant aspects of marriage" before proceeding with his discourse on virginity, and begins his indictment by saying: "Where shall we start, in order to depict this difficult life in the dismal hues that befit it?" And further: "All life's absurdities originate in marriage".[15] The Latin Fathers also — Ambrose and Augustine — follow along the same lines.

Naturally, every so often these same Fathers would remember that they could not go too far down that road without ending up on the side of the very Manichean heretics they were trying to combat in their other writings. Hence we have the occasional reaffirmations of the fundamental goodness of marriage, as when Chrysostom writes ingenuously that "anyone who denigrates marriage also harms virginity"[16], not realizing that he was doing exactly the same thing himself. In this way, virginity was often constructed on the ruins of marriage, which was never the method used by Jesus.

It was a question of a tribute these Fathers were paying to the culture of their day, especially its Neo-Platonic element, which saw the asceticism of the soul as essentially linked to detachment from matter and the flesh, the latter understood in Plotinus' metaphysical sense rather than in Paul's ethical approach. This is not surprising. We too, without realizing it, pay our tribute to the culture whose children we are: a culture with an opposite tendency to theirs — entirely geared to the things of this world as theirs was geared to the things of the next. Our tribute, all in all, is perhaps far more dangerous than the one they paid.

In the vision of these Fathers, the accent moves from eschatology to protology, in other words, from the way things will be at the end, in the heavenly Jerusalem, to the way they were at the beginning, in the earthly paradise. The virgin's model and goal, rather than to live "as children of the resurrection," becomes to live a life free from concupiscence, as before the fall. Rather than an anticipation of the final Kingdom, virginity is seen as a return to paradise. Or rather, the life of the end times is itself conceived on the model of how things were at the beginning, as a "restoration" (*apokatastasis*) of the original state. There is also mention of "the angelic life" (*bios angelikòs*), or "angel-like life," but more in reference to the non-material nature of the angels as pure spirits, rather than in the sense of immortal human beings as Jesus understood it (cf. Mt 22:30).

This same fact can be observed in the case of nearly all the Christian virtues, as I pointed out on another occasion with reference to obedience. The kerygmatic motive, based on the imitation of Christ, is replaced by one derived from Greek ethics, based on the principle of "right reason." Gregory of Nyssa speaks of the soul which "follows reason and remains a virgin."[17] We would have preferred it had he said: "follows Christ's invitation and remains a virgin," but for a long time Christian authors felt the need to find a more universal foundation for virtue, less contingent and historic than the one constituted by the word and example of Christ and the Paschal Mystery. Such a foundation is, or seems to have been, "right reason."

In order to free Christian virginity from the sand-banks where it has on occasion run aground, now that its implied opposition to marriage is no longer accepted, we need to rediscover the simple, natural, biblical motivation that shines out in the very lives of the people of the New Testament: in Jesus, in Mary, in Paul and in John — as well as in the words we have so far examined. All too often the objection is raised that many of the apostles, like Peter, were married men. People forget that, if they were married, the sacrifice which the Lord required of them was even greater: to leave wife, children and homes for the sake of the Kingdom. Peter said: "Look, we left all we had to follow You." And Jesus replied: "Amen, I say to you, there's no one who has left his house or wife or brothers or parents or children for the sake of the Kingdom of God who will not receive many times more in this present age and, in the coming age, life eternal" (Lk 18:28-30).

3. VIRGINITY AND THE PASCHAL MYSTERY

Does this mean, then, that perfect continence for the sake of the Kingdom has no meaning or value from the ascetical point of view? Is it not also sacrifice and renunciation? Certainly it is, but this aspect also needs to be rigorously brought back to its biblical foundation which is "Jesus the Lord" and His Paschal Mystery.

When and how did the Kingdom of God come, and when and how did Jesus become "the Lord"? The apostle Paul himself gives us the answer: on the cross! He became obedient "even unto death, death on a cross. For this reason God exalted Him and gave Him a name above every other name" (Ph 2:8-11). He gave Him the name of *Kyrios*, Lord. I remember the time when some brothers were praying over me for a new release of the Holy Spirit. At a certain point they invited me to choose Jesus as the Lord of my life, freely and consciously. At that moment I happened to look up, and my eyes fell on the crucifix which was on the wall opposite, above the altar. He seemed to have been there for some time, waiting for me. In an instant, this truth branded itself within me: "Make no mistake, this is the Jesus you are choosing as your Lord, not a different, rose-water version!" How often, since then, have I had to admit the truth of those words!

Being espoused to Christ means, here below, being "crucified with Christ," but also in the hope of being glorified with Him. Joy is never absent, but it is a hope-filled joy (*spe gaudentes*). In other words, it is hoping to be happy, and happy to be hoping. "All who belong to Christ Jesus" — writes the Apostle — "have crucified the flesh with its passions and desires" (Gal 5:24). Echoing these words, the martyr Saint Ignatius of Antioch, while on his way to Rome under escort to suffer martyrdom, wrote: "It is a beautiful thing to die to the world for the Lord, so as to rise in Him... Earthly longings (*eros*) have been crucified; in me there is left no spark of desire for mundane things."[18]

40

It is not surprising, therefore, that in the Church's ascetical and mystical tradition the cross has often been defined as the "marriage bed" in which the soul is joined to its divine Spouse. Blessed Angela of Foligno used to say to Christ: "On Your cross I have made my bed." This is the fulfillment of Christ's words: "And when I am lifted up from the earth, I shall draw all people to Myself" (Jn 12:32). On the cross, Jesus draws to Himself the souls who have chosen Him as their Spouse. It is here that the mysterious embrace occurs, of which the Song of Songs speaks: "His left arm is under my head, and his right embraces me" (Sg 8:3). Here too is the fulfillment of the prophetic word we read in Jeremiah: "For the Lord is creating something new on earth: the Woman sets out to find her Husband again" (Jr 31:22). This word refers to the community of the new covenant, seen as God's spouse who will no longer run away from her Husband and chase after idols; rather, she will cling to Him and never be separated from Him again. This event has come to pass, as far as the whole Church is concerned, in what one of the Fathers calls "the ecstasy of the cross," from which the new Eve was born,[19] and which is mystically renewed in each soul who, by betrothing itself to the Crucified One, becomes an image and symbol of the new marriage covenant between God and His people.

This ideal of crucifying one's flesh is certainly not exclusive to virgins (perish the thought!), but is open to all who have received the Spirit of God. Even the married must pass through the fire of Christ's Passover, if they really want their marriage to be the "great mystery" symbolizing the union between Christ and the Church. Where and how did that union between Christ and the Church actually come about? In a bed of pleasures? Or rather, as St. Paul says, "in blood," on the cross? This is why the most complete unity between spouses is experienced not when they enjoy something together, but when they suffer together, each for the other, each with the other, loving each other in suffering and despite suffering. The first unity should serve to make the second possible.

I was saying, then, that to crucify one's flesh is not the exclusive property of virgins. However, it does belong to them under a different and stronger title, because they have made it their way of life. This is where the immense ascetical potential of virginity for the sake of the Kingdom resides, its value in terms of effort, struggle and death. It is no joke to crucify one's flesh with its passions and desires, especially sexual desire, which is among the most imperious of all. The desires of the flesh — self-indulgence — are always in opposition to the Spirit (cf. Gal 5:17). Here we have an unrelenting internal enemy pursuing us day and night, alone or in company. It has an extraordinarily powerful ally — the world — which places all its resources at its disposal and is ever ready to justify and defend its "rights" in the name of nature, good sense, and the fundamental goodness of everything... This is indeed that field "where, the fiercer the daily battle, the rarer the victory."[20] Those ascetical, fiery-spirited monks of the desert had bitter experience of this. Some were brought to the edge of despair by temptations of the flesh. One of them tells his story: "For twelve years, after my fiftieth year, the devil never allowed me a single night or day of respite from his assaults. Thinking that God had abandoned me, and that I was under the Enemy's dominion for precisely that reason, I decided to die an irrational death rather than shamefully yield to the passions of the flesh. I went out, and after wandering through the desert I came across a hyena's den, where I lay down naked during the day, so that the fierce beasts would come out and devour me." After several such attempts, he heard a voice coming from within his own thoughts, saying to him: "Away, Pachon, fight! I arranged for you to be dominated by the Enemy, lest you be proud and think yourself strong. On the contrary, recognize your weakness, place less trust in your rule of life, and turn to God for help."[21]

Today, some look on such ascetical effort with suspicion and call it masochism. We should not underestimate this accusation, but it has no justification when the effort is accepted in freedom, for objective and profound reasons such as those we have mentioned so far. Isn't it true that even someone married to a creature has to struggle and renounce many things, to protect that love and be faithful to it? What, then, is so strange about a man or woman, called to be the spouse of God's majesty, having to face an even more radical and demanding struggle and renunciation?

This is not the place for me to deal at length with specific aspects and practical forms which the struggle for chastity must assume. (I will return to those later.) What is important is to clarify its foundations and the biblical motivation behind it. I said that the ascetical, self-denying component of virginity and celibacy is based on the Paschal Mystery. I believe that this is where the ultimate "why" of virginity and celibacy truly resides. If we understand that, it is an enormous help to overcome many doubts and reservations that have been levelled in history against this state of life — not only outside the Church but, for some time now, also within it. We are now living in a social context where it is no longer possible to rely on external safeguards for the defence of one's chastity, as it was in the past — things like the separation of the sexes, a rigorous filtering of contacts with the world, and all the countless other detailed precautions with which "Rules" usually surrounded the observance of this vow. Unconstrained communications and travel have created a new situation. The defence of one's chastity is now for the most part in the hands of the individual, and it cannot rest on anything other than strong personal convictions, acquired precisely through contact with God in prayer and in His Word. It is in this spirit and with this intention that we continue our reflections.

Celibacy, then, is for the sake of the Kingdom. But why does the Kingdom call for celibacy? Can it not be achieved and manifested completely through marriage, as happened before Christ, in the economy of creation? The answer comes from what Paul writes at the beginning of the First Letter to the Corinthians: "Since, in God's wisdom, the world was unable to come to knowledge of God with its own wisdom, God chose through the foolishness of our proclamation to save those who believe" (1 Cor 1:21). We have here before us a principle of enormous significance which throws light on the whole of Jesus' earthly life, and on the life of every Christian. We know that the "foolishness" of the Gospel proclamation is the cross. From this principle the three religious vows of poverty, obedience and chastity draw their origin and justification. Since human beings have been unable to use their *intelligence* and will to go to God, but have instead made them an idol, it has pleased God to point out a different way, the way of the foolishness of the cross, the renunciation of one's own reason and will, which those who are "fools for Christ's sake" and obedient to Christ use in a different way. Since human beings have been unable to use their sexuality to go out of themselves and open up to the love of God and others, but have made sex an idol which they have even called by name (Astarte, Venus...), it has pleased God to reveal in the Gospel the way of renunciation of the active exercise of sexuality, expressed in continence for the sake of the Kingdom and in perfect *chastity*. Since human beings have been unable to use created goods in *obedience* to God, but have turned them into occasions for greed, robbery and oppression, it has pleased God to reveal in the Gospel the way of renunciation of riches, in radical *poverty* for the sake of the Kingdom.

As can be seen, the ascetical significance of religious vows is based on the living heart of the Christian mystery and on salvation history itself. If Luther in his reform rejected the religious life and vows wholesale, this was only due to external circumstances and to the heat of polemics which prevented a distinction being made between a good thing and the abuse of it. In actual fact, no one ever gave a more solid foundation to religious vows than he did when he formulated the principle that "God reveals Himself in His opposite" (*sub contraria specie*). In other words, in the New Testament God reveals His glory in humility, His wealth in poverty, His wisdom in "foolishness." If in fact God now reveals Himself in a form that is the opposite of what human reason considers appropriate, it follows that one must receive Him as He reveals Himself, enter into His style, speak His language. It would be really strange to try to receive God as though we were wise, rich and joyful, when He reveals Himself as a God who is "foolish," poor and suffering. It is impossible, and Jesus Himself says so when He states that "anyone who wants to come after Me must deny himself, take up his cross and follow in My footsteps" (Mt 16:24; Mk 8:34, 10:21; Lk 14:27), and that the Father "has hidden the mysteries of the Kingdom from the wise and the clever and revealed them to the merest children" (Lk 10:21).

God's second "innovation," which is exclusive to the redemption and gives a privileged place to "foolishness," poverty and chastity, does not cancel out the first innovation, that of creation. In fact the two co-exist even in the new economy of the redemption, where there is a place for intelligence, wisdom and research both in the human and the divine sphere, for marriage and for the possession and use of goods. But the second innovation makes the first one relative and removes from it any claim to be absolute, which leads to idolatry. It places these things in crisis, but it is a salutary crisis from which they emerge purified and brought back to their original forms. St. Gregory Nazianzen was correct when he wrote that "virginity would not exist if there were no such thing as marriage. But marriage would not be holy if it were not accompanied by the fruit of virginity."[22]

Some Fathers of the Church, such as John Chrysostom, Gregory of Nyssa and Maximus the Confessor, thought that if Adam had not sinned there would have been no marriage, with the sexual procreation that is now its distinguishing feature, because in the way in which it is now exercised, human sexuality is the fruit of original sin.[23] However, from a more biblical and less Platonic perspective it must be said that rather the reverse is true: that, had there been no sin there would have been no virginity, because there would have been no need to question marriage and sexuality and subject them to judgment.

Poverty, chastity and obedience are not a renunciation — or worse, a condemnation — of a created *good*, but a rejection of the *evil* that has come to overlay that good. Therefore they are, by definition, a proclamation of the original goodness of created things. They are a way of imitating the Word of God Who, by taking flesh, took on all that belongs to human nature, but did not take on sin (cf. Heb 4:15).

The Gospel counsels, and the vows based upon them, proclaim the goodness and beauty of God's creation precisely by denouncing the ambiguity of human creation. The inability to understand the value of virginity, and likewise of obedience and voluntary poverty, is always a sign that the sense of sin has disappeared from the horizon of faith. It is typical of periods of acute secularization and naive optimism concerning humanity and the world.

Everything we have said so far radically distinguishes Christian asceticism from any other type of asceticism — that of the Gnostics, Manicheans or Cathars — that condemns the actual reality of marriage along with the possession of goods. Seen in this light, poverty, chastity and obedience are the most eloquent proclamation there is of Christ's redemption and of the Paschal Mystery, which does not cancel out the original creation, as the heretic Marcion thought, but "recapitulates" it, as St. Irenaeus said, in other words, brings it out into the light from under the covering of sin. In this light it is also possible to understand the positive element, still valid today, in the Fathers' insight that virginity was a return to the heavenly state, but on condition that this return is not understood as bypassing marriage and human sexuality itself ("male and female He created them"), but only the sin with which they have been overlaid by human freedom.

A virginal and chaste life is therefore in a very profound sense a paschal life. The Apostle writes: "Christ, our paschal lamb, has been sacrificed, so let's celebrate the feast, not with the old yeast, the yeast of wickedness and evil, but with the unleavened bread of sincerity and truth" (1 Cor 5:7-8). The word that is translated as "sincerity" (*heilikrineia*) contains the idea of the sun's brightness (*heile*) and of a test or judgment (*krino*). Therefore it implies a transparency like that of the sun, something that has been tested against the light and found to be pure. This is the model of life that flows from

Christ's Passover, which is common to all Christians but which the virgin must appropriate by a wholly special title, so that he or she becomes its witness and sign for everyone in the Church.

The same basic concept is expressed by Saint Paul in this other exhortation in the Letter to the Romans, where the idea of sacrifice also appears: "I beg you, then, by God's mercy, my brothers, to offer your bodies as a holy and living sacrifice which will be pleasing to God — this is your spiritual worship. Don't pattern yourselves after the ways of this world but transform yourselves by the renewal of your minds, so you'll be able to discern what God's will is — what is good, pleasing and perfect" (Rm 12:1-2). "I beg you then" — the conjunction "then" is significant here. It is saying that the Christian's living sacrifice is required by the sacrifice of Christ, of which the Apostle has spoken previously. The one is the logical consequence of the other. Since Christ has offered His body in sacrifice, so must the disciples offer their bodies as a sacrifice. Here we see that the Christian life, as well as having a paschal character, is also eucharistic.

Sacrifice always presupposes the destruction and death of something, and here too a form of separation and death is mentioned: Christians are not to model their lives on this world, in fact they have to "die to the world." There is a certain analogy between physical death and this ascetical death. In physical death the soul is separated from the body, whereas in this death of the spirit both body and soul, in other words the whole person, separates him or herself from the world, which for the person represents a kind of larger body in which they live and move. Both deaths are painful because they involve uprooting ourselves from the ground in which we were planted and raised. This is why Paul speaks of a "living" sacrifice. It is a dying by living, and a living by dying. As the Apostle says, it really is a crucifixion: "The world has been crucified to me, and I to the world" (Gal 6:14).

Once again, we must be very careful not to think of this ideal of a living sacrifice as something belonging exclusively to virgins. Let us just say that virgins are obliged to own it and to live it in a more radical way, making it the substance of their daily life. They must not let themselves be led into error if they often hear the traditional ideal of "flight from the world" being challenged today as no longer corresponding to our idea of a Church which is "for the world." The expression may be open to criticism and perhaps may need to be dropped, but its substance is unassailable because it rests on the Word of God, which is alive and everlasting. St. John, who had written in the Gospel that "God loved the world so much," is the same one who writes to Christians in his first letter: "Do not love the world, or what is in the world" (1 Jn 2:15).

To conclude this first part, in which I have tried to highlight the biblical motivations underlying virginity, I would like to quote a passage from the decree of Vatican Council II on the renewal of religious life, which summarizes nearly all the motives we have mentioned: "Chastity 'for the sake of the Kingdom of Heaven,' which religious profess, must be esteemed as an exceptional gift of grace. It uniquely frees the human heart (cf. 1 Cor 7:32-35) so that one becomes more fervent in love for God and for all people [the *existential* dimension of virginity]. For this reason it is a special symbol of heavenly benefits [the *prophetic* dimension of virginity], and for religious it is a most effective means of dedicating themselves wholeheartedly to the service of God and the works of the apostolate [the *missionary* dimension of virginity]. Thus for all Christ's faithful religious recall that wonderful marriage made by God, which will be fully manifested in the future age, and in which the Church has Christ for her only Spouse [the *spousal* dimension of virginity]."[24]

PART TWO

How to Live Virginity
and Celibacy for the Sake
of the Kingdom

1. MATRIMONY AND VIRGINITY: TWO CHARISMS

In our day, celibacy or virginity has become an institution in the Church. As far as society is concerned, it is a "state," and in fact our identification cards say: Civil Status — "bachelor," "single," or "unmarried." So, it is a state now regulated by laws. Within the Church celibacy is the subject of endless debate (should it, for example, be maintained or abolished for priests, and so on). Outside it, it has been viewed with suspicion and sometimes with pity by many representatives of the so-called human sciences, such as psychology and sociology. One of these — to quote the most famous of all — said that "in our age, neurosis has taken the place of the convent, which used to be the refuge of all who had been let down by life or who felt too weak to face it."[25] According to this view, virginity and celibacy were the ancient equivalent of modern neurosis!

In such an atmosphere it is very likely that the words "celibacy" and "virginity" immediately bring to mind the idea of an unresolved problem, a "burning issue," rather than an ideal, a divine "innovation" by Christ Himself. There is a danger of losing sight of essentials and concentrating on accidental matters which are merely side-issues. What is needed, therefore, is a change of mind, a conversion, and this can only happen by the work of the Holy Spirit. He does not do new things, but makes things new. He renews persons and institutions, even including celibacy for the sake of the Kingdom and virginity for love of the Lord. The Holy Spirit is moving powerfully in the Church, giving everything in it a new authenticity and evangelical splendor. I never grow tired of quoting the words of John Paul II, written on the occasion of the sixteenth centenary of the ecumenical Council of Constantinople (381 A.D.), which proclaimed the divinity of the Holy Spirit: "*The entire work of renewal in the Church*, which Vatican II so providentially proposed and initiated... cannot be fulfilled except *in the Holy Spirit*, that is, with the help of His light and His strength."[26]

What actually is virginity, either for men or for women? Starting with a word from St. Paul, which we commented on earlier ("Regarding those who are unmarried, I have no directions from the Lord, but I give my own *opinion*" [1 Cor 7:25]), the preference in the past was for virginity — like voluntary poverty and obedience — to be viewed and explained in terms of "evangelical counsels." As such, they were different from "precepts," such as conjugal fidelity for example. I believe that whatever could be said and understood about virginity using such a concept has been amply illustrated already, and there is very little new to add to the clear synthesis St. Thomas makes in his *Summa*

Theologica.[27] This is why it may perhaps be useful for us to try to see what new understanding can be derived by starting from another category the Apostle uses, in the same context, to define marriage and virginity: the category of a *charism.* "All," he says, "have their own gift (charism) from God, one of one sort, another of a different kind" (1 Cor 7:7). In other words, married people have their charism and virgins have theirs. Besides, the idea of a "gift" is implicit in the words Jesus Himself uses to institute celibacy for the sake of the Kingdom, when He says that not everyone can understand this proposal, but only those to whom it is granted (*dedòtai*; cf. Mt 19:11).

"A manifestation of the Spirit"

If therefore virginity is essentially a charism, then it is a particular "manifestation of the Spirit," because that is how a charism is defined in the New Testament (cf. 1 Cor 12:7). If it is a charism, then it is more a gift received from God than a gift given to God. Jesus' words: "You haven't chosen Me; on the contrary, I have chosen you" (Jn 15:16) apply to virgins in an altogether special way. You do not choose celibacy and virginity in order to enter into the Kingdom, but because the Kingdom has entered into you. In other words, you do not remain a virgin to save your soul more easily, but because the Kingdom, or rather the Lord, has taken possession of you, chosen you, and you feel the need to remain free to respond fully to that choice.

From everything we have said so far we can already begin to see the need for a conversion in connection with virginity and celibacy. This conversion consists in moving from the attitude of someone who thinks they have given a gift or made a sacrifice, a big sacrifice, to the quite different attitude of someone who is aware of having received a gift, and a great gift, and needs most of all to give thanks. We must admit that sometimes that feeling is present in consecrated persons, at a more or less conscious level. Sometimes our married brothers and sisters encourage such a view without realizing it, by comments like: "What a sacrifice, what courage it takes to give up the chance to have your own family and live alone, to give up such a brilliant future and lock yourself up in a seminary or a convent!" And possibly we end up believing it ourselves. Whereas if our vocation is genuine we know that precisely the opposite is true and that they ought to exclaim: "How fortunate!" I believe that there is no one called to this way of following Christ who at some time — especially at the beginning, when the vocation begins to blossom — has not clearly seen, or at least glimpsed, that what they were receiving was for them the greatest grace of God, after Baptism.

Now let us take a step forward. If virginity or celibacy is a charism, then it must be lived charismatically, and to live it *charismatically* means, quite simply, living it as one usually lives a gift. First of all, with *humility.* The great martyr Ignatius of Antioch, living very close to the apostolic era, wrote: "If a person manages to live in chastity in honor of the Lord's flesh, let him live it with humility, because if he boasts of it he is lost, and if he considers himself greater than a bishop he is ruined."[28] Some Fathers, such as St. Jerome, St. Augustine and St. Bernard, even said "better an unchaste, humble person than a proud virgin." There is a great affinity between humility and chastity, just as there is between pride and lust. Lust is carnal pride and pride is spiritual lust. Celibates and virgins are particularly exposed to the temptation of pride. They are people who have never knelt to a creature, or recognized their incompleteness and their need for another person by saying: "Give me your being, because my own is not sufficient for me!" "Man — it has been said with profound truth — is a proud being. There was no way to make him understand his neighbor, except by making that neighbor enter in to his flesh. There was no way to make him understand dependency, necessity and need, except through the law of submission to another, for no other reason than that the other exists."[29] The first and most radical form of submission is that of man to woman and of woman to man. In a different, non-conjugal way, celibates and virgins also live this form of submission, which is so valuable for overcoming self-sufficiency, pride and independence. But they are certainly less "conditioned" by the other sex and therefore more exposed to the spirit of pride. A visitator sent by the ecclesiastical authorities to a certain community of very austere and cultured virgins (I think it was the famous Port Royal community) had occasion to write in his report: "These women are as pure as angels, but as proud as demons."

So, the first way to live the gift of chastity is humility. The second is *joy and peace*, because it is written that "the fruit of the Spirit is love, joy and peace" (Gal 5:22), and, if perfect chastity for the sake of the Kingdom is a "charism," it must manifest the fruits of the Spirit.

Finally, if virginity is a charism it must be lived with *freedom*, because again it is written that "where the Spirit of the Lord is, there is freedom" (2 Cor 3:17). Interior freedom, obviously, not exterior: it means the absence of complexes, taboos, embarrassment and fear. Certainly, great harm was done to Christian virginity in the past by surrounding it with a great mass of fears, suspicions and warnings: "Be careful of this, watch out for that!", thereby turning the vocation into a kind of highway where all the road signs read: Danger! Danger! This is a repetition of the mistake made by the lazy servant in the Gospel who, having received a precious talent, is afraid to lose it, so he goes off and buries it rather than making it bear fruit. We have allowed the world to think that the principle at work in *it* is stronger than the principle at work in us, whereas St. John tells Christians clearly: "He Who is within you is greater than the one who's in the world" (1 Jn 4:4). At times we really have put the lamp "under the bushel" when it should be put on the lampstand to give light to all who are in the house, in other words, in the Church.

We have seen that virginity for the sake of the Kingdom is both a paschal detachment from the world and a prophecy about the future life. In the past, religious men and women chose to give witness, through the color and cut of their habits and by other signs, especially in their renunciation of the world and their separation from it. Wouldn't it be a fine and timely thing if some new religious communities — and the traditional ones, too, in some way — also showed the world the other, more important, aspect of their charism: the fact that they are an anticipation, in faith and hope, of the shining joy of the heavenly Jerusalem, when the bride will wear a robe of "fine linen, pure and bright" (cf. Rv 19:8)? Such witness, so positive in its eloquence of a different beauty and a different joy which do not decay, is perhaps more necessary for the world than the negative testimony which speaks of flight from the world, even if it is good to remember that the best witness to this joy is the light in one's eyes and the unction of one's speech, rather than the color of one's clothes.

But perhaps the most important result of speaking about virginity and celibacy in terms of charism is that the latent opposition between virginity and marriage, which has so beset both Christian vocations, is finally laid to rest. Virginity is a charism, and marriage is a charism too. Both are therefore particular "manifestations of the Spirit." How can they be incompatible or opposed to each other, if both come "from the same Spirit"? In the notion of a charism, and that of vocation, which is closely related to it, the two forms of life can finally be fully reconciled and can even strengthen one another. The one confirms the other, it does not destroy it. Precisely because in the Christian view marriage is considered to be something good, and a spiritual gift, so, for that very reason, virginity and celibacy are beautiful and noble. Indeed, what merit would there be in not marrying, if marriage were something bad or simply dangerous and inadvisable? To abstain from it would be a duty and nothing more, like abstaining from any occasion of sin. But precisely because marriage is good and beautiful, the renunciation of it for a higher motive is even more beautiful. A person who goes to listen to a fine concert is doing something good and wholesome, but if, even though they really wanted to go, they forgo the concert out of love — for example, so that they can be close to someone they love and help them feel less lonely — it is an even better thing. In this sense Paul says that "the one who marries does well; and the one who doesn't marry does better still" (cf. 1 Cor 7:38).

When you think about it, it is only the existence of marriage that makes virginity a choice, and only the existence of virginity that makes marriage a choice. Without either of them there would no longer be any "choice," or, if there were (as between marriage and so-called free love, or getting married and staying single solely for the sake of freedom and an undisturbed life), it would be morally unacceptable.

In saying this we are not saying anything new and revolutionary, but are only correcting a certain conditioning bound up with particular cultures and historical moments, and getting back to the ideas and attitudes of Jesus. The Holy Spirit never ceases to guide the Church, in every area, to a knowledge of the complete truth. "By the working of the Holy Spirit" said St. Irenaeus, "revelation, like a precious liquor in a valuable container, constantly renews its youth and also makes the container grow younger."[30] The Holy Spirit — as I said above — does not do new things, but makes things new. He makes them young again, restores them to their original splendor, and He does the same with the charism of consecrated virginity.

On the subject of getting back to the spirit and thought of Jesus, I have been very struck by the fact that in Matthew's Gospel, immediately after the sayings of Jesus about those who do not marry for the sake of the Kingdom of Heaven, come His words about children — without any break, in fact linked to them by a temporal adverb: "Then (!) children were brought to Him so He could lay His hands on them and pray, but the disciples rebuked them. Jesus said, 'Let the little children come to Me'" (Mt 19:13-14). In this way, Jesus' words about voluntary chastity are enclosed between two major sayings of His about marriage: one regarding the indissolubility of marriage ("Haven't you read that He Who created them from the beginning made them male and female… ?"), the other about children. Children are the fruit of marriage; they are the love of the two spouses made flesh. To welcome children, as Jesus does, is to welcome in the fullest way and in its most profound implications, the reality of marriage. To say "Let the little children come to Me" is like saying "Let the spouses, let the fathers and mothers, come to Me." Parents know very well that to welcome their children is to welcome them, in fact it is more. Naturally, all this is true when the marriage itself is lived in faith and in harmony with the will of God.

Only in faith do the two charisms meet and shed light on one another. This is why the martyr St. Ignatius of Antioch, whom we heard warning virgins to be humble, admonishes married people in the same text to marry "in the Lord." "It is proper," he writes at the beginning of the second century, "that spouses should enter their union with the bishop's consent, so that the wedding takes place according to the Lord and not according to concupiscence, and that everything is done for the honor of God."[31] Everything is always brought back to the same source, the lordship of Christ. Virginity has value if it is embraced "for the Lord," and matrimony has value if it is celebrated and lived "according to the Lord."

"For the common good"

But let us advance still further in our teaching about charisms. A charism — says St. Paul — is a particular "manifestation of the Spirit given to each one for the *common good*" (1 Cor 12:7). St. Peter says the same thing when he writes "to the extent that each of you has received a gift (*charisma*), use it to serve one another as good stewards of God's varied grace" (cf. 1 P 4:10).

What does all this mean when we apply it to our case? It means that celibacy and virginity are also for the married, and that marriage is also for virgins, in other words for their benefit. Consecrated virginity, therefore, is not a private matter, a private choice of perfection. On the contrary, it is "for the common good" to be used "to serve" others. The gift is destined only for some, for those who are called, but all are its beneficiaries. Such is the essential, apparently contradictory nature of a charism. It is something specific and individual — "a manifestation of the Spirit given to each one," but at the same time it is something which is to be placed at the service of all ("for the common good").

In the Church, virgins and married people mutually "edify" one another. The married are reminded by virgins of the primacy of God and of the things that do not pass away. They are introduced to love of God's Word, which consecrated persons, having more time and being more available, are able to study in greater depth in order to "break" the bread of the Word for their brothers and sisters who are more taken up with the occupations of the world.

But virgins and celibates also learn something from married people. They learn to be generous, to forget themselves, to serve life and often to have a certain humanity that comes from direct contact with the events of life. I am speaking from experience. I belong to a religious Order where until a few decades ago we used to get up at night to pray the Office of Matins, which lasted about an hour. Then came the great upheaval in religious life in the wake of the Council, partly positive and partly less so. It seemed (not without reason) that the rhythm of modern life, study for the younger friars and apostolic ministry for the older ones, now made it impossible to interrupt our sleep and rise during the night hours, and gradually the practice was abandoned almost everywhere. However, as the years went by the Lord introduced me to many families in the course of my ministry. I particularly remember a group of these young families, with children constantly arriving in one or another of them. I then discovered something which came as a salutary shock to me: those young mothers and fathers had to get up not once but five, six or more times a night to feed or nurse or rock a crying child, or watch at its bedside if it had a fever. And in the morning, at the same time each day, one of the two, or both of them, having taken the child to a grandparent or to the nursery, would rush to work in time to clock in, come rain or shine, good health or sickness. Then I said to myself: if we don't do something about it, we are in grave danger here! Our lifestyle, unless it is supported by a genuine observance of the Rule and by a certain rigor in its schedule and customs, is in danger of becoming a rose-water existence which will eventually make us uncaring. Do we have the right to feel offended when someone calls us "parasites"? We certainly do have that right, but only if we spend ourselves unreservedly for the Kingdom, if we are truly "united to the Lord without distractions." Otherwise, we have no such right.

What good parents are able to do for their children according to the flesh, the degree of self-forgetfulness they are capable of attaining in order to provide for their children's health, studies and happiness, must be the measure of what we ought to do for our spiritual children who are our brothers and sisters in the Lord. Our example in this is the apostle Paul himself, who said he wanted to "spend what he had and to be spent" for the sake of his children in Corinth (cf. 2 Cor 12:15).

This shows how useful it is that there should be a healthy integration of charisms in the Christian community, whereby married people and celibates do not live in strict separation from one another, but in such a way that they can help and encourage one another to grow. It is not true that the proximity of the other sex and of families is always necessarily a danger or a dark threat for the unmarried. It can be, if one has not yet accepted one's vocation freely, joyfully and definitively, but this is true for a married person too. Today we are called to work pastorally in a society no longer organized along the lines of the separation of the sexes, but one where both sexes constantly interact and are present together in every area of life and work. We need to adapt the way we live our charism to this new situation.

In no way does this mean that each person has to give up his or her own lifestyle and surroundings. In the earliest days of the Church, virgins and celibates — as we can deduce from Paul, Tertullian, Cyprian and others — were integrated into Christian homes as part of the fabric of the whole community. But very soon, certainly by the fourth century, they felt the need for a place apart where they could organize their time, with its rhythm of silence and activity, in accordance with their own special vocation. And so monasteries were born, like those founded by St. Ambrose in and around Milan.

Today new types of community are coming into being, in which families and consecrated persons live together in the same location and share the same rule of life. Together they profess and practice poverty and obedience. The one thing that distinguishes them is whether they are married or celibate. This manifests an important aspect of the Church: the fact that it is a body with "many members," each different from the other yet moved by one and the same Spirit (cf. 1 Cor 12:12-27). In this particular form of life there is a need on both sides for space and freedom. The married need it in order to attend to their children, join in their games, solve the inevitable family tensions and cultivate mutual love. Virgins need it in order to cultivate silence and study, and to be "united to the Lord without distractions."

While respecting the lifestyle of each, there are many ways in which married people and celibates can be spiritually united within a community. I once attended a meeting of the clergy and pastoral councils of a local Church and I remember the spiritual boost, the joy and the unity caused by the reading of a letter from the cloistered nuns of a convent in the same diocese, by which they showed they were present at the meeting, contributing to it through their prayers.

2. HOW TO CULTIVATE THE CHARISM
OF CELIBACY AND VIRGINITY

I spoke earlier about the freedom one must have in living the charism of virginity. We also need to say something about how one arrives at that freedom, and about the price to be paid. In fact, one of the greatest dangers to guard against in this whole area is precisely the danger of delusion. After sin, sexuality is no longer a neutral reality which we can easily dominate. It has become ambiguous. The Bible is familiar with this ambivalent, dramatic character of sexuality. It knows that passion is capable of dragging a person to ruin: "For love is strong as death" — we read in the Song of Songs — "passion as relentless as Sheol" (Sg 8:6). The Old Testament is full of dismal stories in which individuals or entire cities appear as victims of the devastating power of sexual disorder.

It is true that Jesus came to redeem humanity and therefore also human sexuality. It is also true that "condemnation will never come to those who are in Christ Jesus" (cf. Rm 8:1). But redemption has not exempted human beings from concupiscence and the need for struggle. Certainly Jesus redeems and saves human sexuality, but He redeems and saves it as He does with everything else, through the cross, in other words, by calling us to share His struggle, so that we can later share His victory. When Israel entered into possession of the Promised Land, it is

70

written that "the Lord allowed these nations to remain; He did not hurry to drive them out, and did not deliver them into the hands of Joshua" (Jg 2:23). The Lord did subject to Israel the nations who occupied the land of Canaan, but not all of them, and not all at once. He allowed some to remain, in order to put Israel to the test by their means, and to teach Israel the art of war (cf. Jg 3:1 ff.). He has done the same with us in Baptism. He has not taken away all our enemies, our temptations; some, our appetites, He has left with us, so that we would learn to fight and to hope in Him, and experience our weakness.

Mortification

Christ, then, did not eliminate the concupiscence of the flesh in us, but He has given us the means not to give in to it. The first and most common means available to us to preserve and increase virginity of the heart is mortification. St. Paul assures us: "If by the Spirit you put to death the deeds of the body, you'll live" (Rm 8:13). This is spiritual mortification, where "spiritual" does not mean an internal type of mortification, as opposed to an external, bodily one, but mortification that is both external and internal, practiced with the help of the Holy Spirit. In short, a type of mortification that is not itself a work of the "flesh," but of faith.

For a soul that wants to be the spouse of Christ, mortification is necessary, just as, in the case of a human love, it is necessary to learn the language of the beloved. "Consider," writes the philosopher we have already mentioned, who remained celibate for love of the divine majesty, "a purely human situation. If a lover is unable to speak the language of the beloved, then he or she must learn the other's language, however difficult it may be. Otherwise their relationship could never become a happy one; they would never be able to converse with each other. So it is with mortifying oneself in order to love God. God is spirit: only a mortified person can in some way speak His language. If you do not want to mortify yourself, then you cannot love God either. What you are speaking of is something quite different from Him."[32]

Speaking of mortification, I think these days we must particularly insist on that of the eyes. "The eye is the lamp of the body," Jesus says. "Now if your eye is clear, your whole body will be filled with light. But if your eye is not, your whole body will be darkness" (Mt 6:22-23). In a civilization dominated by images, as ours is today, images have become the privileged vehicle of the ideology of a world saturated with sensuality, which has made human sexuality its favorite theme, detaching it completely from the original meaning given to it by God. Today, healthy fasting from images has become more important than fasting from food. Food and drink, in itself, is never impure, but certain pictures and images are. St. John places "disordered desires of the eyes" (1 Jn 2:16) among the three fundamental appetites, and St. Paul in turn exhorts us to "keep our eyes on what is unseen rather than on what can be seen, for what can be seen is transitory but what is unseen is eternal" (2 Cor 4:18).

Visible things exert their formidable power of seduction over us precisely by making us forget that they are transitory. Their beauty is such that they appear, to a spirit still enslaved by matter, to be everlasting, although we can see with our own eyes that they wither and decay from one day to the next. St. Augustine, who was all too familiar with this struggle against the lure of material things and of deceptive beauty, can help us with his testimony: "Behold, You were within me but I was outside, and it was there that I searched for You. In my unloveliness, I plunged into the lovely things which You created. You were with me, but I was not with You. Created things kept me from You; yet if they had not been in You, they would not have been at all... I resist the allurements of my eyes, lest they entangle my feet... What countless seductions have men added to the things which entice the eyes, through the various arts and the works of craftsmen, in the form of clothes, shoes, vessels, and other artefacts of this kind, even in paintings and all sorts of representations — these things far overreach the bounds of necessary utility, moderation and faithful representation... Now I, who am speaking and seeing these things clearly,

get my steps entangled in these beautiful things…
yet You pluck me out in Your mercy."[33]

The best way to overcome the seductive power
of images is not to "fix our gaze" on them, not to
become "enchanted" by them. If you look at them,
they have already won a victory over you. That, in
fact, was all they wanted from you: that you would
look at them. "Avert my eyes from pointless images," we are taught to pray by one of the psalms
(Ps 119:37). The benefit derived from such mortification of the eyes is wonderful indeed! Through
it we really can experience something of that ideal,
so dear to the Fathers of the Church, of a "return
to paradise," to a time when all was pure and fresh
and crystal-clear, as on a summer's morning, "and
the youthful body was so chaste that its manly gaze
had the depths of a lake."[34]

The motivation "for the sake of the Kingdom
of Heaven" is precisely the reason why we — especially we priests — are required to have this commitment to keep our eye and our whole body "in
the light," as Jesus says. When brothers or sisters
come to us, struggling, weak and tempted by the
flesh, they expect to find a safe hand to help them
out of the quicksands of sensuality. But to do this we
need to have our feet on solid ground, otherwise we
will tend to be drawn in after them ourselves. We
are now seeing the spread of a repulsive impurity
that threatens the very sources of human life. The
Church, today as in the past, needs people who are

austere with themselves, humble but sure of the inherent strength of grace, to oppose this flood of "debauchery, desire, revelry, carousing, and disgusting idolatry" as Scripture calls it (cf. 1 P 4:4), which is rushing the world to ruin. Today this is one of the most urgent services we must render, not only to the Kingdom of Heaven but to society itself. The "quality of life" truly is at stake!

But what help can we give, if we ourselves are defiled, or worse still engulfed, by those quicksands? I believe that no motives of prudence or closing of ranks should silence the cry that is rising from the heart of our Mother the Church. If we have no qualms about denouncing the sins of others and of society, we should be equally frank in denouncing our own. There are too many priestly lives compromised, too many failures, too much depletion of energies in the Church, caused by the weaknesses of priests in this area! My brother priests, we should with fear and trembling act quickly to put things right, as far as is necessary, because great is God's pain and anger over these things. It is written that our God is a "jealous God" (cf. Ex 20:5). Who are we to defy God's jealousy? We are the "friends of the Bridegroom," and this title should fill us with joy, but also with a holy trepidation and with infinite respect for souls. It is a kind and blessed mortification of the flesh, that gains for us, with the Holy Spirit's help, the grace of being truly "fathers," our hearts free to love everyone without wanting to possess anyone. No price should seem too high to us, for a vocation that someone has summarized in the following words: "To live in the midst of the world, with no desire for its pleasures; to be a member of every family, yet belonging to none; to share all sufferings, to penetrate all secrets, to heal all wounds; to go daily from men to God, to offer Him their homage and petitions, to return from God to men, to bring them His pardon and His hope; to have a heart of iron for chastity and a heart of flesh for charity; to teach and to pardon, console and bless and to be blessed for ever. O God, what a life is this, and it is thine, O priest of Jesus Christ."[35]

Healthy knowledge and acceptance of sexuality

A healthy *knowledge* and *acceptance* of the sexual component of our life is also a valuable aid to living our charism peacefully. Human sexuality, as we now know, is not confined to procreation alone, but is reflected in the person in a vast range of potential expressions, some of which are fully valid also for celibates and virgins. Celibates and virgins have renounced the active exercise of sex, not sexuality itself. Certainly they have not gotten rid of it. It is still there, and it pervades practically every expression of the personality. A virgin man does not cease to be a man, nor a virgin woman to be a woman.

This fact is also recognized by psychology, which admits the possibility of "sublimating" the sexual instinct without destroying it, but spiritualizing it and making it serve ends that are equally worthy of humanity. The sublimation process can be ambiguous if it is unconscious and directed towards the creation of substitutes, but it can also be positive and a sign of maturity if it is motivated by ideals and lived out in freedom. In this sense we can say that there is a dimension of *sexuality* also experienced by celibates, and a dimension of *celibacy* that is often experienced by married men and women.

A healthy knowledge of sexuality helps us develop a calm, untroubled view — as far as this is still possible in our present situation, compromised as it is by sin — of the whole of created reality, including the transmission of life. We must learn how to look at the opposite sex, at procreation, and at children, with pure eyes, in short, with eyes like those of Jesus Who, as the Gospels show, was able to speak about these things in perfect freedom and even turned them into parables about spiritual realities. A proper knowledge of the life of married people helps us to avoid wrong or simplistic ideas about marriage, trains us to be healthily realistic (so necessary for anyone who has to preach the word of God), opens our eyes to the many advantages we have compared to married people, and makes us more understanding and attentive to their problems.

Finally, a certain lucidity in this area is useful so that we do not mistake the flesh for the spirit, or

vice versa, the spirit for the flesh — either in ourselves or in those we are called upon to guide. In
other words, it is useful for spiritual discernment.
We mistake the flesh for the spirit when we take as
supernatural and divine love, or spiritual friendship,
what in fact are only the beginnings of human love.
Human and "carnal" love, in its initial stages, pro-
duces effects that are easily mistaken for the effects
of grace and conversion of heart. The face lights up,
the person becomes sweet-tempered and compliant,
feels generous and helpful and experiences a new
idealism and fervor. As I was saying, it is easy to think
one is dealing with conversion of the heart, when
in fact it is only the beginning of a human falling in
love which can have unfortunate consequences if it
is not immediately recognized as such. A religious
may believe that, as a result of meeting him or her,
a certain person has been transformed. So the religious is pleased, and insists on seeing, writing to or
telephoning the person. They may even thank God
for having been chosen as His instrument. The truth
is that God has been at work, but in quite a different
way. He allows all this to bring us out of delusion and
presumption and to make us humbler and wiser for
the experience.

On the other hand, we mistake the spirit
for the flesh, that is, good for evil, when we do
not know how to distinguish temptation from sin.
Choosing virginity does not spare a person from
temptations. In fact, as we see from the lives of the

saints, it often increases them. The Desert Fathers used to say that no one should think they possess a certain virtue, until it has been tested in the fire of temptation. But temptation in itself is not bad. It is for our good, since we know that "along with the temptation, God will also provide a way out, so you'll be able to endure it" (cf. 1 Cor 10:13). "It is better for many not to be altogether free of temptations, but to be often assailed, lest they become too secure, and run the risk of pride, or take more liberty to seek after exterior consolations."[36] Temptation is the crucible in which chastity is purified, the cold bath in which it is toughened, as steel is tempered by contact with water.

If the Enemy continues to make war against you, this might mean that he has still not obtained what he set out to achieve, otherwise he would stop tormenting you. If you experience struggle in your flesh, it means you have not surrendered, otherwise you would immediately be at peace (I am referring, of course, to a false peace). If you have no struggle at all, rather be afraid and question yourself. Recognize that either this has happened by a free gift of God — in which case you should simply thank Him and feel unworthy of it, or else it has happened because you have become accustomed to evil and compromise — in which case it is time for you to wake up.

St. Catherine of Siena once received a visit from her heavenly Spouse at a time when she was being assailed by a tide of temptations of the flesh. "My Lord," she called out to Him, "where were You when my heart was being tormented by so many temptations?" And the Lord replied: "I was in your heart." And she said: "Saving always the truth of what You say, my Lord, and with all due respect for Your Majesty, how can I believe that You were living in my heart, when it was full of unclean and devilish thoughts?" And the Lord answered: "Those thoughts and temptations: did they gladden your heart, or sadden it? Did they bring you pleasure or displeasure?" And she replied: "Great pain, and great displeasure." And the Lord answered: "Who was it Who made you feel displeasure, if not I Who was hiding in the center of your heart?"[37]

What is said about temptation applies also, in a different way, to the simple "call" of the other sex. No-one should be surprised or over-anxious if at certain times the appeal of the other sex, and for men, the fascination of women, are strongly felt. This is not evil, it is simply natural. It goes back to the fact that "from the beginning, God made them male and female." We must not hide behind the screen of "angelism," or seek refuge in coarse language, in order to show off our freedom with the other sex, when freedom is precisely what is missing. Nor do we need to make demons of the other sex, especially of women, or scorn and insult beauty simply because it is "visible" and "transitory." Beauty, as we know, comes from God, even if it can be wrongly used. Since in the past, in this and in every other area, things were always seen from a man's point of view, it is not surprising that the ambiguity of sex, which we mentioned earlier, was translated into ambiguity about women and into misogyny. Not even the Bible, in so far as it reflects a particular culture, is entirely immune from it. See, for example, the Book of Sirach (25:12 ff.): "Any spite, rather than the spite of a woman! ... Do not be taken in by a woman's beauty... Sin began with a woman, and thanks to her we must all die." In this way anything shady or destructive about sexuality is identified with women. From companion and "helper" similar to man, woman then becomes his shame, an obscure threat and a trap. But this comes from sin, not from God.

Instead, what we should do is turn that "call" and fascination of the other sex into the best part of our "living sacrifice." We should tell ourselves: "Fine, this is exactly what I have chosen to offer for the sake of the Kingdom and for the Lord!" And if at certain times, especially in youth, that call is transformed into temptation, we should launch bravely into battle with the name of Jesus in our heart and on our lips, as brave soldiers sometimes go on the assault, shouting the name of their sovereign or their captain above the fray.

I would also like to say a word in this connection about the delicate question of physical or external virginity, and about spiritual or interior virginity. The Church has always honored virginity, even in its physical and bodily manifestation, calling it "holy virginity" (*sancta virginitas*). Clearly, it is not virginity itself that is "holy," since it is possible to remain virginal and intact for many reasons which have nothing to do with holiness. What enables us to speak of holiness in this case is the intention or purpose that moves a person to remain a virgin.

Sometimes people may have made the mistake of overvaluing the physical aspect of wholeness, both in men and women. A certain contemporary culture, as I remarked at the beginning, has reacted by going to the opposite extreme by denying virginity any value at all, even making it a figure of fun.

Basing ourselves on the Word of God, what can we say? St. Paul told us earlier that the unmarried woman, the virgin, gives her full attention to the Lord's affairs "and to being holy in body and spirit" (1 Cor 7:34). To be a virgin only in body means little or nothing; to be a virgin in spirit is a fine thing; but to be a virgin "in body and spirit" is very beautiful indeed. In such a case, the sign and its meaning meet and complete each other, as do nature and grace. For such as these, the Book of Revelation reserves the singular privilege of "following the Lamb wherever He goes" (cf. Rv 14:4), making them the symbol of those absolutely faithful souls who have never compromised themselves with idolatry.

We must therefore encourage those consecrated souls who, without any merit of their own, of course, but by God's gift, have managed to preserve their purity and are able to offer an integral gift to God. In actual fact there is, in this, an altogether special hint of God's glory which is not to be found anywhere else, because — as our friend the poet says — "That which has been regained, defended every inch, retaken and won back, is not the same as what was never lost. A sheet of whitened paper is not white; a whitened fabric is not white; a human soul is never quite as white, when whitened, as it would be, white."[38]

It is not a question of a taboo, as unbelievers think, or of a simple privilege or honor of which whoever has it is usually proud. Rather, when it is freely accepted, what is involved is a delicate and profound sacrifice, one which calls to mind the primordial sacrifice God asked for from His creatures, that they should give up the will to know "good and evil" personally and by experience. In fact it is one thing to give up the use of sex and bodily pleasure after having experienced it, and another (much more demanding) to renounce the wish to experience it. That means accepting that there is an experience, basic to other men and women, which you freely choose not to want to experience, for love of the Lord. Only God knows the fragrance of this sacrifice, which touches not just the heart or the body, but the very being of the creature.

Having said this, however, it must also be said that spiritual virginity is the most important, and that it is not something given once and for all and to be preserved, but rather something that can be acquired day by day. By His grace, God has transformed some of the greatest sinners into His most loving and most loved spouses. This is why anyone who has lost physical integrity and baptismal innocence, for whatever reason, does not need to spend his or her consecrated life constantly looking back and brooding over past failures and mistakes in every detail. This only makes the situation worse, like a woman walking with a jar of water on her head: the more tense she is and the more she thinks about it, the more water she spills.

On the contrary, what is necessary is to strive to grow in interior virginity, letting go of the useless desires and affections in our hearts, because purity of heart can restore a new virginity to the soul. In a certain sense, virgins are not born, they are made. This does not mean that one can calmly accept any situation and wait for it to improve. On the contrary, if a person has not yet managed to eliminate from his or her life habits that are seriously contrary to chastity, and has not achieved a certain balance and mastery in the sexual sphere, it is still a good rule to advise the person against making a definitive commitment to celibacy or virginity.

Precisely because the essential virginity is that of the heart, the way of virginity is in some way open to all, even to those who are or have been married. If there are some "who do not marry for the sake of the Kingdom of Heaven," there are others who, for the same reason (i.e. for the sake of the Kingdom of Heaven), do not re-marry, though they could do so. There is a certain kind of widowhood, devoted to the family and to good works, that has always been highly honored in the Church and placed immediately after virginity.

In this connection I would also like to say a word about another human situation: people who, for a whole variety of possible reasons, have been unable to marry, though they would have liked to do so. They did not choose their situation. In fact, it may cause them great suffering. To them I would like to say this: Jesus tells us that some are eunuchs because they are like that from birth, others are made so by human agency, others again have made themselves so "for the sake of the Kingdom of Heaven." Apparently, you belong to the first or second category. But, in the sight of God, no one is irredeemably condemned, or a prisoner of situations. In other words, it is possible to pass from one category to another: from the category of those who have not married because of the circumstances of life, to the category of those who do not marry "for the sake of the Kingdom of Heaven." You need only accept the situation as something allowed by God, reconcile yourselves to that way of life and use your greater freedom to devote yourselves to prayer and to the Gospel cause. In this way you too can share in the "hundredfold" promised by Christ to those who leave everything to follow Him. The greatest in the Kingdom of Heaven are not those who belong to the "more perfect state," but those who love and suffer most. This is why they can move ahead of so many others whose lives, apparently, were more successful.

Community

One final aid to living virginity for the sake of the Kingdom which I would like to mention, is *community*. Men and women are "relational beings." Relationships constitute the person (as we say today), just as in the Trinity it is the "relationships" (of the Father to the Son, of the Holy Spirit to the Father and the Son, etc.) that constitute the three divine "Persons." No-one can live and grow harmoniously without real and deep inter-personal relationships. Community is often precisely what constitutes our "hundredfold" in this life. When it is healthy and genuine, community enables us to have (and to be) fathers, mothers, brothers, sisters, sons and daughters.

Friendships too with people of the other sex (which can easily become a danger if they are cultivated exclusively and furtively) are a great gift, if they are shared in some way with one's community.

For some time now, new forms of celibacy and consecrated virginity have come to exist in the Church, known as "secular institutes." Their members each live in their own home and environment, yet the fact of sharing the same spirituality and observing the same rule, and the strong human bonds between them, reinforced by the days and weeks they spend together during the year, can be for them the equivalent of a community.

On the other hand, there is a question about diocesan priests and pastors who live entirely alone. Is this a suitable situation in which to live celibacy? I believe we must have the courage to face up to this problem. The very example of secular institutes today shows that it is possible to achieve a type of community and communion without living together under the same roof. The natural community where a diocesan priest finds nourishment and support, and is also challenged when necessary, is the "presbyterium." When this ministry first appeared in history, alongside bishops and deacons, the term indicated the community of presbyters gathered around their bishop — a community which the martyr St. Ignatius compares to the college of apostles gathered around Jesus.[39]

Every reform of the clergy has felt the need to tackle this problem, by creating forms of common life for the clergy, some of which are still actively functioning today. A presbyterium whose members know one another, who cultivate the bonds of brotherhood established during the years spent together in the seminary, who meet for monthly retreats and spiritual exercises, together with their bishop, and who exchange news and experiences, especially in these days of easy communications, is already a form of community which must be strengthened at all costs.

3. THE VIRGIN MARY

Jesus' words about celibacy for the sake of the Kingdom are preceded, as often happens in the Gospel, by the fact. And the fact is Jesus Himself, Who not only remained a virgin but was also born of a virgin mother. After Jesus, called by the Fathers "the Arch-Virgin" (*Archipàrthenos*)[40], there is Mary, whom the Church calls "the Ever-Virgin" (*Aeipàrthenos*).

"The angel Gabriel was sent from God… to a virgin" (Lk 1:26). Notwithstanding all the discussions, the words are there, in the Bible, firm as a rock. Exegetes point out that on this point Luke's account depends on the prophecy of Isaiah 7:14: "The virgin is with child, and will give birth to a son." This is true, but it changes nothing, in fact it heightens the importance of the Gospel account by demonstrating its long prophetic preparation and rootedness in the history of salvation. It is the literary presentation of the fact, the account of the event, which depends on Isaiah, not the event that is recounted. If in fact, behind the *account*, there had not been a new event that actually happened, why would the evangelist and the Christian community have thought of that very prophecy, which (at least in the Septuagint text) contained the idea of virginity, so foreign to the Jewish mentality of the time? Why not copy, for example, the mode of Isaac's birth — much more acceptable and biblically convincing — or that of Moses or some other Old Testament celebrity? The answer is given: in order to mark Christ's difference and superiority over any other man who came before Him. But that is something we can say, after the event, and the Fathers did say so from the second century onwards, once the superior value of virginity for Christians had been affirmed. But the community in which this account was formed was not yet in a position to say so. It did not yet have the elements to enable it to give precedence to virginity — especially in its feminine version — over marriage. To suppose, already in this initial stage of the Christian faith, a knowledge and influence of pagan myths about the miraculous births of the gods, would be altogether artificial and without foundation.

The most important thing to note is, therefore, not that the Gospel account depends on the prophecy of Isaiah, but that both the account and the prophecy depend on a certain event that God had first pre-announced and later accomplished in the fullness of time. I have never understood those biblical scholars who recognize the prophetic value of the Old Testament as a proclamation of and preparation for the New, but who then refuse to recognize any such prophetic character in any actual text, including this text of Isaiah, which the Gospel itself explicitly relates to the birth of Christ from the Virgin Mary (cf. Mt 1:23).

At the dawn of the new times, Mary, in her virginity, embodies the new form of life which has been made possible precisely by the coming of the Kingdom. One could see a symbolic significance in the encounter between Mary and Elizabeth in the Visitation. Elizabeth, representing the Old Testament economy (Mt 11:13: "For all the Prophets and the Torah up to John prophesied"), was married; Mary, representing the New Testament economy, is a virgin.

In Mary appears all the splendor of the biblical motivation for virginity, expressed in the words "for the sake of the Kingdom of Heaven" and "for the Lord." She was chosen; the Kingdom "overcame" her, took possession of her, and she let herself be possessed. Jeremiah would say: she let herself be "seduced." St. Paul is the man "set apart for the service of the Gospel" (Rm 1:1); Mary is the woman singled out and set apart for the Author of the Gospel. I believe that the idea of a "vow" of virginity taken by Mary, apart from being biblically unfounded, actually diminishes rather than enhances Our

Lady's virginity, because it would then depend more on the personal initiative of a creature than on the sovereign and free initiative of God. It would therefore be an ascetical practice, rather than a work of grace. Mary did not "find favor with God" because she was a virgin; she was a virgin because she had found favor with God, and she was chosen so that through her the beginnings of the Kingdom on earth would be uncontaminated. Certainly Mary responded perfectly, with absolute faith, to the call to virginity. She accepted all its consequences joyfully and without discussion, saying: "Here I am!" She thus became the model for all the countless hosts of young men and women who, through the centuries, were to receive the same call to be "virgins and mothers," "virgins and fathers."

After the title of *"Theotokos"* (Mother of God), that of "Ever-Virgin" is the one by which Mary is most often invoked by the liturgy, both Latin and Orthodox. The latter, in its finest Marian hymn, the *Akathistos*, never tires of greeting her with this refrain: "Hail, Virgin Spouse," invoking her as the model and protector of virgins:

> "Hail, mother and nurse of virgins!
> Hail, you who lead souls to the Bridegroom!
> Hail, Virgin Spouse!"

Saint Gregory of Nyssa brings out the profound affinity that exists between Mary and every Christian virgin, which in turn is based on an analogous relationship to Christ. He writes: "That which came about physically in Mary Immaculate, when the fullness of Godhead shone in Christ through virginity, is also repeated in every soul who follows reason and remains a virgin, even though the Lord no longer makes Himself materially present."[41]

Mary is not only the model but also the "advocate" and protector of virgins. She does not confine herself to pointing out the way of virginity, but helps them to follow it by her intercession and watchful care. Saint Basil writes: "Just as clear and transparent bodies, when struck by a ray of light, themselves become resplendent and reflect a different ray, so do those Spirit-bearing souls, enlightened by the Holy Spirit, themselves become fully spiritual and shed grace over others."[42] Mary is, quintessentially, the "Spirit-bearing" soul, bearer of the Holy Spirit; she is the shining body who casts light over others. So true is this that even Luther was obliged to write of her: "No image of woman gives a man such pure thoughts as this virgin does."[43]

Mary is truly a unique creature, the "blessed one among women." All other women in the Church are either virgins physically and mothers spiritually, or physically mothers and spiritually virgins. She alone is both, in other words physically and spiritually both "virgin and mother." God could choose no more eloquent language than this by which to honor both marriage and virginity, and to make us accept both as His handiwork. These two charisms, coming "from the same Spirit," before dividing into two categories of persons in the Church, found themselves united in Mary, who is the first cell and model of the entire Church. Thus, no state of life in the Church is deprived of the glory of having, in Mary, its own beginnings and model, and no state of life can boast of imitating Mary by itself, with no need of the other. "All creatures," writes the poet we met earlier, "lack something. Those who are carnal lack purity. [Instead of "carnal" and "pure," read "virgin" and "mother," and all will be clear.] She, on the contrary, lacks nothing, because, though carnal, she is pure. But, though pure, she is also carnal. So it is that she is not simply a woman unique among all women. She is a creature unique among all creatures. Literally the first, after God."[44]

I have spoken about the means to be used to cultivate the charism of celibacy and virginity. Constant attention and devotion to Mary is certainly one of the simplest and most effective.

CONCLUSION

We have based our words about virginity on the fact that it is first of all a charism, a gift received from God and, consequently, a vocation. But just as in the Mass we offer to God the bread and wine we have received "through His goodness," so that the gift received may become a gift offered to God's majesty, so must virginity, received as a gift, become an offering to God's majesty, a living sacrifice and imitation of the Eucharist of Christ. A great spiritual teacher of ancient times wrote: "The Fathers were not content to observe the commandments, but also offered God gifts. I will explain how: Christ's commandments have been given to all Christians, and every Christian is obliged to observe them. One could say that they are the taxes due to the king. If anyone were to say: 'I will not pay my taxes to the king,' could he escape punishment? But there are in the world some great and famous men who not only pay the king's taxes but also offer him gifts and deserve great honors, great gifts and great dignities. And so the Fathers also not only observed the commandments but offered gifts to God. Virginity and poverty are gifts. Nowhere is it written, in fact, 'Thou shalt not take a wife, thou shalt not have children'."[45]

The most beautiful thing we can do as we conclude our meditation is to renew this gift of ourselves, offering to God once more our "Here I am!" through the hands of Mary. What makes a gift beautiful and precious is its integrity. The object we give must be new and intact. No one would dream of giving a friend a worn-out thing or a half-eaten apple. In these matters one has to be tactful, not just concerned about the "substance." In other words, we must not take back from Christ anything of what we have given Him. We must allow nothing in ourselves — in thoughts, looks, or actions — to offend His presence or "grieve" the Spirit.

In any love-story there are usually two stages or phases. There is the initial stage, where love is expressed by the giving of gifts, especially the gift of self. Then there comes a time when it is no longer enough to give gifts to the beloved, but one has to be ready to suffer for her or for him. Only then can it be seen whether the love is real. In the story of a vocation to consecrated virginity there are also usually two stages. There is the initial stage of the vocation, when, spurred on by grace and attracted by the ideal, one joyfully and enthusiastically says, "Yes, Lord, here I am!" Then comes the time of solitude of heart, of weariness, of crisis, when, in order to maintain that "Yes," one has to die. The prophets speak of such a painful experience in our relations with God. "I remember your faithful love, the affection of your bridal days, when you followed Me through the desert," says God in the prophecy of Jeremiah (Jr 2:2). In the Book of Revelation, the risen Lord addresses a Church in these words: "You have lost your first love" (Rv. 2:4), the love you had in the beginning.

Our great hope is that, though our former fervor may have diminished, grace never fails, the Lord's right arm "is never shortened." In such cases it is good to gather all one's strength and say, a second and a third time, like the young Samuel:

"Here I am, as You called me" (1 S 3:1 ff.). Shall we do it? The surest way is to "re-choose" Jesus as the Lord and Spouse of our soul. When we do this, something similar happens as in the life of a young man or woman when they really fall in love. While they were "free" and open to various possibilities, any boy or girl who passed by might have drawn their attention and "distracted" them, just as a sheep always leaves a scrap of its wool on the thorns of a hedge when it comes too close. But once true love for someone has taken hold, every other person, and in fact the whole world, respectfully steps back and even fades away entirely for a while. Their hearts are now fixed on one person. A kind of catharsis happens: the new relationship does not destroy all others—companions, relatives or friends — but puts each one in its proper place. Something similar happens to the consecrated soul on the day when, moved by the uncreated love which is the Holy Spirit, he or she chooses Jesus as Lord and Spouse. The heart is no longer "free," no longer wanders, and is no longer so easily "distracted" this way and that.

This is true virginity for the sake of the Kingdom. God grant that we may desire it, even if from a distance, and make our way towards it, albeit haltingly, with the steps of a child.

FOOTNOTES

[1] *Babylonian Talmud*, Jabamot 63 a.

[2] St. Cyprian of Carthage, *On Virgins*, 22; PL 4, 475.

[3] J. Rivière - P. Claudel, *Correspondance*, Paris 1926, pp. 261 f.

[4] O. Rank, in E. Becker, *The Denial of Death*, New York/ London, 1973, p. 173-4.

[5] Clement of Alexandria, *Pedagogue*, I, 6.

[6] B. Isaac of Stella, *Sermon* 51; PL 194, 1863.

[7] St. Gregory Nazianzen, *Poems* I, 2; PG 37, 523 A.

[8] *The Ancrene Riwle*, Part I: The Divine Service.

[9] S. Kierkegaard, *The Journals*, XI A 154.

[10] *Genesis Rabbah*, 34, 14a (Simeon ben Azzai).

[11] St. Augustine of Hippo, *Confessions*, X, 29.

[12] St. Gregory of Nyssa, *On Virginity*, 5; SCh 119, p. 336 f.

[13] St. Gregory of Nyssa, Ibid., 3.

[14] cf. G. van der Leeuw, *Phänomenologie der Religion*, Tübingen 1956, ch. 2-29.

[15] cf. St. Gregory of Nyssa, *On Virginity*, 3-4.

[16] St. John Chrysostom, *On Virginity*, 10; SCh 125, p. 122.

[17] St. Gregory of Nyssa, *On Virginity*, 2; SCh 19, p. 268.

[18] St. Ignatius of Antioch, *Letter to the Romans,* 2 & 7.

[19] St. Methodius of Olympus, *Symposium on Virginity*, 3, 8; PG 18, 73A.

[20] St. Caesarius of Arles, *Sermon* 41, 2; CCL 103, p. 181.

[21] Palladius, *Lausiac History,* 23, ed. G.J.M. Bartelink, Milan 1974, pp. 129 ff.

[22] St. Gregory Nazianzen, *Oration* 37, 10; PG 36, 293 C.

[23] cf. St. John Chrysostom, *On Virginity*, 17, 5; St. Gregory of Nyssa, *The Creation of Man*, 16; PG 44, 181 ff.

[24] Vatican II, *Decree on the Renewal of Religious Life* (*Perfectae caritatis*), 12.

[25] Sigmund Freud, *Five Conferences on Psychoanalysis*, 1909.

[26] AAS, 73, 1981, p. 521.

[27] cf. St. Thomas Aquinas, *Summa Theologica*, I-IIae, q. 108 a. 4.

[28] St. Ignatius of Antioch, *To Polycarp*, 5, 2.

[29] Paul Claudel, *The Satin Slipper*, III, sc. 8.

[30] St. Irenaeus, *Adversus Haereses*, III, 24, 1.

[31] St. Ignatius of Antioch, *To Polycarp*, 5, 2.

[32] S. Kierkegaard, *The Journals*, X, A 624.

[33] St. Augustine, *Confessions*, X, 27 & 34.

[34] Charles Péguy, *Eva, Oeuvres Poétiques*, Paris 1975, p. 944.

[35] H. Lacordaire, quoted by D. Rice, *Shattered Vows*, The Blackstaff Press, Belfast 1990, p. 137.

[36] *Imitation of Christ*, I, 20.

[37] Blessed Raymond of Capua, *Life of St. Catherine*, XI, 110.

[38] Charles Péguy, *Le mystère des saints Innocents*, Oeuvres Poétiques, p. 804.

[39] cf. St. Ignatius of Antioch, *Letter to the Magnesians*, 6, 1.

[40] cf. St. Methodius of Olympus, *Symposium* I, 4; PG 18, 44C.

[41] St. Gregory of Nyssa, *On Virginity*, 2.

[42] St. Basil, *On the Holy Spirit*, XI, 23.

[43] M. Luther, *Sermon on the Christmas Gospel* of 1522, Ed. Weimar, 10, 1, p. 68.

[44] Charles Péguy, *Le porche du mystère de la deuxième vertu*, *Oeuvres Poétiques*, p. 575 f.

[45] Dorotheus of Gaza, *Teachings*, I, 11-12; SCh 92, p. 164.